NEMEA

A GUIDE TO THE SITE
AND MUSEUM

As of this writing, the hours of the museum
are those of the site: 8:45 A.M. to 3 P.M.
Tuesday through Saturday and 9:30 A.M. to
2:30 P.M. on Sunday. The museum is closed
on January 1, March 25, Orthodox Easter,
and December 25. On December 24 and December 31 it is open from 9 A.M. to 1 P.M.
and on Good Friday from 9 A.M. to noon.
Sunday hours are in effect on January 6, Ka-
theri Deutera (the Monday forty-eight days
before Easter), the Saturday before and the
Monday after Easter, May 1, the feast of the
Holy Spirit (the Monday fifty days after
Easter), July 26, August 15, October 28, and
December 26.

THE TEMPLE OF ZEUS AT NEMEA *CA.* 1805,
FROM W. GELL, *THE ITINERARY OF GREECE*
(LONDON 1810) PL. 2 (DETAIL)

NEMEA

A GUIDE TO THE SITE
AND MUSEUM

EDITED BY STEPHEN G. MILLER

WITH CONTRIBUTIONS BY

ANA M. ABRALDES, DARICE BIRGE,

ALISON FUTRELL, MICHAEL GOETHALS,

LYNN KRAYNAK, MARK LANDON,

AND JEANNIE MARCHAND

UNIVERSITY OF CALIFORNIA PRESS

BERKELEY   LOS ANGELES   OXFORD

UNIVERSITY OF CALIFORNIA PRESS
BERKELEY AND LOS ANGELES

UNIVERSITY OF CALIFORNIA PRESS, LTD.
OXFORD, ENGLAND
© 1990 BY
THE REGENTS OF THE UNIVERSITY OF
CALIFORNIA

Library of Congress Cataloging-in-Publication Data

Nemea: a guide to the site and museum / edited by
  Stephen G. Miller ; with contributions by Ana M.
  Abraldes . . . [et al.].
      p. cm.
  Bibliography: p.
  Includes index.
    ISBN 0-520-06590-5 (alk. paper). — ISBN
  0-520-06799-1 (pbk. : alk. paper)
    1. Nemea Site (Greece)—Guide-books.
  2. Greece—Antiquities—Guide-books. I. Miller,
  Stephen G. (Stephen Gaylord), 1942–
  II. Abraldes, Ana M.
DF261.N45N45   1989
938'.6—dc20   89-4942

Printed in the United States of America
1 2 3 4 5 6 7 8 9

The paper used in this publication meets the
minimum requirements of American National
Standard for Information Sciences—Permanence
of Paper for Printed Library Materials, ANSI
Z39.48-1984.

CONTENTS

ILLUSTRATIONS

PREFACE AND ACKNOWLEDGMENTS

The antiquities of the ancient Greek world, scattered through-out the regions surrounding the Mediterranean and Black seas, are best known from the sites where the Greeks lived, worked, worshiped, and played. Some of those sites have never been excavated; others have been more or less thor-oughly investigated. None is completely excavated. None has yielded its last secrets.

At Nemea less than half of the ancient site has been un-covered. Thus a guidebook that offers an overview of the site and its history may well be proved wrong the next time the pick goes into the ground. Nonetheless, Nemea—like many other sites—has by now given enough of itself that we may offer such a guide with some confidence in its accuracy. Moreover, it is in the very nature of human knowledge that corrections and additions often are (and should be) required; this will undoubtedly be true at Nemea.

What we now know of Nemea has resulted directly from excavations by the University of California at Berkeley which have taken place since 1974 under the direction of the under-signed. It has also resulted from the efforts of many individu-als, most of them connected with the University, during that period. These individuals, too numerous to list here, can be found in the first footnote of every preliminary report in the journal *Hesperia* (see the Bibliography). They have made real contributions to our understanding of Nemea, frequently in difficult conditions.

This book is likewise the result of a cooperative effort. A group of graduate students at the University of California, past and present, have made direct contributions: Ana M. Abraldes, Dr. Darice Birge, Alison Futrell, Michael Goethals, Dr. Lynn Kraynak, Mark Landon, and Jeannie Marchand are listed in the Contents at the entries that each of them wrote. (The remaining entries were written by the undersigned.) This list, however, does not reveal how the editing process, largely the responsibility of the undersigned, benefited from the careful reading of each contributor and the lively discussions to which each contributed. Professors Mary Sturgeon, Homer Thompson, and David Young and James Clark, Director of the University of California Press, made useful suggestions. The text has been improved substantially by the careful copyediting of Stephanie Fay. The design is the work of Laurie Anderson. Other members of the University of California Press staff have also been helpful, particularly Jane McKinne, Steve Renick, and Deborah Kirshman. In addition, the drawings of Martha Breen (Figs. 31, 35, 41, 53, 60, 64, and 65) and Katerina Sklere (Fig. 54) help us to understand the ancient situation.

The American School of Classical Studies at Athens, under whose aegis and on whose behalf the University of California at Berkeley has worked at Nemea, is to be thanked and congratulated for its help with the Nemea project. When the Managing Committee of the American School resolved in December 1968 that Nemea should be a priority of the School, the process began the results of which are embodied in this book.

Finally, the Ephoreia of Antiquities at Nauplion, the Archaeological Service of Greece, and the Ministry of Culture have all worked closely with the University of California and the American School in the excavations at Nemea. The visitor enjoying the museum and the archaeological park at

Nemea benefits from the work of these institutions and their representatives.

Stephen G. Miller
February 2, 1989

TO THE READER

In our effort to achieve a satisfactory middle ground between a technical and detailed guidebook to Nemea for scholars and a more general guide for other visitors, we offer definitions of technical terms at their first appearance in the text. With the aid of the index, these definitions can easily be found again.

Notations consisting of a letter or letters followed by a set of numbers refer to the permanent inventory system by which each artifact is uniquely identified in the Nemea system. BR 671, for example, is the 671st artifact inventoried in the BR[onze] category; A 100 is the 100th artifact inventoried in the A[rchitecture] category; SS 8 is the 8th artifact in the S[tone] S[culpture] category, and so forth.

We hope that you may read this guide at Nemea, beginning perhaps at the marble picnic tables at the entrance to the site or on the benches on the porch of the museum. We wish you a happy visit to Nemea!

I

INTRODUCTION

Greece has given us many traditions and concepts which were first developed more than two thousand years ago in this small and rugged land. Here man first learned how to portray himself and his surroundings in a realistic way, not only in the media of stone, clay, bronze, and paint but also in words, seeking to understand both the observable phenomena of nature and the abstractions of his own psyche. Here, too, he developed, defined, and put into practice such political systems as oligarchy and democracy. And he experimented with another political idea: that differing political entities might voluntarily unite for the good of all at the expense of their own supposedly conflicting interests. In antiquity, this idea was first expressed in the form of Panhellenic athletic festivals and their accompanying truces.

For part of every year, a Panhellenic truce was in effect, and representatives of the whole Greek world assembled to celebrate the temporary cessation of their squabbles and the recognition of their common tongue, gods, and culture. The focal point of these festivals was the athletic competitions, but with the athletes and their trainers came poets and sculptors, pilgrims and politicians, magicians and pedlars, and ordinary citizens looking for a good time. Gradually these festivals gave rise to the idea of a "United Nations of Greeks," to the idea that it might be possible to stop wars and collaborate in the face of other, common, enemies. This idea became a political reality, however, only under the force of Macedonian arms in 338 B.C.

Nemea should be understood against this background, for it was not a habitation center but a Panhellenic site, like Olympia, Delphi, and Isthmia, where periodic influxes of tens of thousands of visitors alternated with quiet times when only a very small permanent population of priests and caretakers remained.

The Panhellenic Cycle

Of the four festivals, the one at Nemea was the youngest. Olympia, according to ancient records, became the site of a Panhellenic festival in 776 B.C., Delphi (where the Pythian Games took place) in 586 B.C.,[1] Isthmia in 580 B.C., and Nemea in 573 B.C. These games were the four *stephanitic,* "crown," games where the victors' only award was a wreath: olive at Olympia, laurel at Delphi, wild celery at Nemea, and pine originally and again later at Isthmia, with dry celery during the Classical and Hellenistic periods.[2] These four games were distinguished from other, local, festivals, where cash prizes were given to the victors. These four festivals stood apart not only for their prizes and for the Panhellenic truce but also for the preeminence of their athletic competitions. A man who won at all four games was especially honored as a *periodonikes,* "circuit winner."

The cycle of the games covered a four-year period, but the games at Olympia and Delphi were quadrennial, whereas

---

1. On the accuracy of this date as opposed to 582 B.C. (the date generally accepted by earlier scholars) for the beginning of the Pythian Games, see S. G. Miller, "The Date of the First Pythiad," *CSCA* 11 (1978) 127–58.

2. See O. Broneer, "The Isthmian Victory Crown," *AJA* 66 (1962) 259–63.

those at Isthmia and Nemea were biennial. The evidence suggests that the cycle was as follows (note that the Greek year began at the summer solstice):

Solar Year 1, July/August: Olympic Games (e.g., 480 B.C.)

Solar Year 2, July/August: Nemean Games (479 B.C.)

Solar Year 2, April/May: Isthmian Games (478 B.C.)

Solar Year 3, July/August: Pythian Games (478 B.C.)

Solar Year 4, July/August: Nemean Games (477 B.C.)

Solar Year 4, April/May: Isthmian Games (476 B.C.)

Solar Year 5, July/August: Olympic Games (476 B.C.)

Although the Isthmian Games were in the same years as the Olympic and the Pythian games by our time reckoning and could be considered as a "warm-up" for the latter two games, for the ancient Greeks the Isthmian Games fell in the same year as the Nemean Games. Thus each of the two quadrennial games had a whole solar year reserved to it, but the two biennial games shared their solar years. One result of this cycle is easily seen in the records of the best ancient athletes, which usually list about twice as many victories at Isthmia and Nemea as at Olympia and Delphi. Nonetheless, the glory and value of a victory at Isthmia or Nemea seem not to have been diminished, for an Athenian law of around 430 B.C.[3] provided that a man who had won at Olympia, or Delphi, or Isthmia, or Nemea would receive free meals at state expense for the rest of his life. Moreover, Pindar seems to have accepted with equal willingness commissions to write odes honoring the victors at any of the four sites.

The Program

The basic program at Nemea seems to have been more like that at Olympia and less like that at either Delphi or Isthmia,

3. *IG* I³, 131.

with an emphasis on purely athletic events and an exclusion, at least originally, of musical contests. The following competitions were included in the Nemean program:

A. THE GYMNIC EVENTS[4]

Stadion. A straight sprint from one end of the track in the stadium to the other, a distance of 600 ancient feet or, at Nemea, nearly 178 m. (see p. 176).

Diaulos. A double *stadion* race, probably run in individual lanes, down and back up the track to finish at the starting line (about 355 m. total at Nemea).

Hippios. A double *diaulos* race four lengths of the track, or about 710 m.[5]

Dolichos. A long-distance race whose total length the sources give variously as 7, 10, 20, or 24 lengths of the stadium track.[6] The evidence, at least for Olympia, slightly favors the 20-length distance, which would make the *dolichos* about 3,600 m., or roughly 2¼ miles.

Hoplitodromos. A race the length of a *diaulos,* but with the competitors carrying bronze shields and wearing helmets and, originally, metal greaves on their shins.

Pyx. An event in some ways like modern boxing, but with significant differences. The competitors bound their hands and wrists with long leather thongs that protected their knuckles and strengthened their wrists but also damaged their opponents. There were no weight divisions and no rounds, and the judges' only duty was to prevent fouls. The victor was decided either by knockout or by one competitor's acknowledging defeat.

---

4. Gymnic events were so called because those who competed in them were *gymnos,* "nude."

5. This race seems to have been held only in the Isthmian and Nemean Games, and not always even in these; see Pausanias 6.16.4.

6. J. Jüthner, *Die athletischen Leibesübungen der Griechen* (Vienna 1968) 108–9 and n. 232, collects and discusses the ancient sources.

Pankration. Much like the *pyx* in the method of deciding the victor, but a combination of wrestling and boxing with no holds barred except biting and gouging. This brutal event more than once ended with the death of one of the contestants; competitors specialized in such maiming tactics as breaking fingers as well as in strangleholds, and other deadly stratagems.

Pale. An event in which, unlike modern wrestling, the opponents wrestled only from an upright position, the object being to throw one's opponent to the ground within an area apparently marked off by a layer of sand or dust. Three clean throws of the opponent were needed for a victory.

Pentathlon. A five-part competition consisting of a *stadion* and a wrestling, or *pale,* bout (both like the individual events described in the preceding paragraphs); the throwing of the javelin (*akon*); the hurling of the discus (*diskos*); and a long jump (*halma*). In antiquity the javelin, discus, and long jump events existed only as parts of the pentathlon. Although the winner of this event would emerge clearly when only two men competed, it is not known how the winner was determined in a larger field. Several different systems (point, round-robin, and so forth) have been proposed in modern times,[7] but the ancient evidence is inconclusive. Because of its combination of demands on the contestants' speed, strength, endurance, and coordination, the pentathlon was a great favorite of the ancient philosophers', but the most famous athletes of antiquity were only rarely pentathletes.

B. THE EQUESTRIAN EVENTS

The equestrian competitions took place in a hippodrome. The winner was the owner, not the jockey or charioteer, who

---

7. For the debate on systems of scoring with references to earlier scholarship, see H. A. Harris, "The Method of Deciding Victory in the Pentathlon," *G&R* 19 (1972) 60–64; R. Merkelbach, "Der Sieg im Pentathlon," *ZPE* 11 (1973) 261–69; and J. Ebert, "Noch einmal zum Sieg im Pentathlon," *ZPE* 13 (1974) 257–62.

was usually a slave or a servant. Women, men, and even city-states could own horses. Only by way of such ownership could "national" teams participate in the games and women, at least before Roman times, compete in them. No ancient hippodrome has ever been found in Greece, and the evidence for its length is inconclusive. Thus only approximate, relative distances for the races are given in the list that follows.

Tethrippon. A four-horse chariot race over a distance of 8,400 m., or 5¼ miles.

Synoris. A two-horse chariot race over a distance of 5,600 m., or 3½ miles.

Keles. A horseback race over a distance of 4,200 m., or 2½ miles.

In addition to the physical challenge, the equestrian events had a psychological handicap. This took the form of a frightening place in the hippodrome where the horses ran amok, thereby adding excitement to the competitions. At Nemea there was a red rock in the hippodrome which accomplished this goal, perhaps by means of reflected light.[8]

C. THE MUSICAL EVENTS

The musical competitions known at Delphi and Isthmia, including those in flute and lyre playing and in singing to the accompaniment of the lyre, were not part of the Nemean Games before the Hellenistic period (or the Olympic Games before the Roman period), by which time the games were at Argos (see p. 57). Two nonathletic events were held at Nemea and Olympia that cannot, however, be termed musical competitions:

8. Pausánias 6.20.19 attests to the phenomenon of the red rock at Nemea as well as to the tomb of a hero at Isthmia and another at Olympia which served the same purpose. The Olympian version was called *Taraxippos* (Pausanias 6.20.15–18), "horse frightener." The effectiveness of such "obstacles" probably derived from a myth-inspired anxiety in the charioteer which was transmitted to the horses.

Keryx. A competition for heralds in which strength and clarity of voice were rewarded. To the winner, in addition to the wreath of victory, went the privilege of announcing the events and the winners for the gymnic and equestrian competitions.

Salpinktes. A competition for trumpeters in which the goals appear to have been strength, clarity, and duration of sound. The winner signaled when each gymnic and equestrian event was about to take place.

These gymnic, equestrian, and musical events made up the complete program of the games. Although in the "heavy" events of boxing, wrestling, and the *pankration* there were no weight classes, in all the gymnic events competition was by age group: boys (12–16 years); *ageneios,* "beardless youths" (16–20); and men (21 and over). In an era without birth certificates, passports, and drivers' licenses, the *Hellanodikai,* "judges," would frequently categorize competitors by physical maturity rather than by chronological age. The other function of the *Hellanodikai* was to enforce the rules of training and competition; fouls were punished by flogging with long sticks or switches.

The competitions included neither team events nor contests judged by subjective criteria and scored according to point systems (except the musical events, whose different rules may explain why they were not popular at Nemea and Olympia). Ancient Greek athletic competitions were as intensely individualistic as the society whence they came.

The Festival

The length of the games at Nemea is unknown, but the Olympics were held over a period of five days, with the athletes assembling a month earlier to train under the watchful eyes of the *Hellanodikai.* A similar schedule probably existed at

Nemea, and the larger crowd would gradually assemble during the time before the games. By the beginning of the games (perhaps the second full moon after the summer solstice), thousands of visitors would have arrived. The valley would have been filled with tents and temporary hutches, stalls for pedlars, a continual din of animals and of human voices, and smoke from a thousand campfires and from the sacrifices performed almost continuously at the Altar of Zeus. A week later the roads leading from Nemea would have been filled with crowds of people sated with food, drink, and the competitions. In the valley only caretakers would have remained to clean up, sculptors to erect commissioned statues of recent victors, and poets to seek inspiration for odes celebrating those fresh victories. The stalls of the pedlars, so thick a few days earlier, would have disappeared, and magicians and philosophers would have gone to display their sleight of hand and mind to new audiences.

The modern visitor should try to envision such scenes at Nemea. The goal of the excavations is not only new insights into ancient architecture, sculpture, painting, numismatics, and the other physical remains of antiquity but also a better understanding of the ancient athletic festivals and the vicissitudes of the Panhellenic idea. As will emerge in the pages which follow, the evidence so far uncovered in the excavations tells much, and it reveals that the history of Panhellenism was not always a rosy one. We are forced, in the end, to confront the fact that man did not, at least in Classical Greece, learn to live in harmony with his neighbor unless he was compelled to do so.

The Setting

Nemea is situated in an upland valley in the eastern foothills of the Arkadian mountains (Fig. 1). A visitor entering the valley rarely realizes that the Sanctuary of Zeus at the valley's center is some 333 m. above sea level. This height and the prevailing west winds off the mountains combine to keep the valley relatively cool during the summer months and damp and chill during the winter, when frosts, ice, and snow are common. The valley is fertile and well watered, and its vineyards and olive groves give it a verdant hue even in the heat of summer. This relative cool of temperature and of vision, compared to that of most of Greece, may have played a role in the ancient selection of the site for Panhellenic festivals which took place at the height of summer.

The low ridges surrounding the valley are punctuated by higher peaks. At the southeast is Evangelistria Hill (surmounted by a modern church), in the slopes of which the 4th-century B.C. Stadium was constructed. Until 1989 the main road into the valley from the east skirted the northern slopes of the Evangelistria Hill, bisecting the Stadium. A new road is being built along the southern and western flanks of the hill, and its completion will create a new entrance into the valley. A series of shallow caves that the local inhabitants identify with the home of the Nemean Lion can be seen near the top of Evangelistria Hill. No ancient remains have ever been noted in or around these caves.

The southern end of the valley is marked off by a lower ridge which overlooks the Argive plain further south. The southwestern corner of the valley is accentuated by the rugged scarps of Mount Daouli (Fig. 2). Near the center of a ridge along the western side of the valley is the peak of Prophetis Elias and the chapel dedicated to him. In antiquity this hill was known as the Trikaranon, "three-headed." In the valley beyond this ridge lies the ancient city-state of Phlious. The ridge continues northward to the peak of Stimanga, which rises on the western side of a narrow gorge at the northern end of the Nemea valley. This gorge is the point of egress for the Nemea River in its journey from the valley to the Gulf of Corinth. On the eastern side of the gorge, dramatic and distinctive, stands the flat-topped Mount Phoukas (the ancient

Apesas and the site of an altar of Zeus Apesantios).[9] The top
of Phoukas, which affords a magnificent view of the whole
northeastern Peloponnesos, is approached by a dirt road along
the southern scarp of the mountain, at the southwestern corner of which is an abandoned monastery which can be used as
a shelter for overnight stays. (There is neither electricity nor
water, however.) Phoukas marks the northern end of a ridge
which runs along the eastern side of the Nemea valley and
separates it from the territory of the ancient city-state of
Kleonai. From the top and the eastern side of this ridge the
stone for the Temple of Zeus and many other buildings at
Nemea was quarried (see pp. 133–34).

The Nemea valley is thus relatively long and narrow, being
only about a mile at its greatest east-west width. With the
gorge at its northern end, it forms a funnel for the north wind
which sweeps through it, especially during the winter; trees
are scarce in the central corridor of this funnel. The center of
the valley is marked by a low ridge which stands out like an
island west of the Sanctuary of Zeus. This is the Tsoungiza Hill.

The modern village, at the center of the valley and grow-
ing up the southern and eastern slopes of Tsoungiza, is officially named Archaia Nemea but is commonly called Herakleion. It has about 450 residents, two general stores, one
gasoline station, a coffee house, a sometime restaurant, and
a church. About three miles west, in the valley of ancient
Phlious, is the town of Nea Nemea, which the visitor must be
careful to distinguish from Archaia Nemea. Nea Nemea has
a population of more than 5,000 and serves as the supply center for the whole region. Between Archaia Nemea and Nea
Nemea is the hamlet of Koutsomadi, on the southeastern
slopes of Prophetis Elias. In the valley some three miles east
of the valley of Archaia Nemea is the town of Archaiai Kleonai
(commonly called Kondostavlo), with some 1,200 inhabi-

9. The altar is mentioned by Pausanias (2.15.3), who attributes its founding
to Perseus.

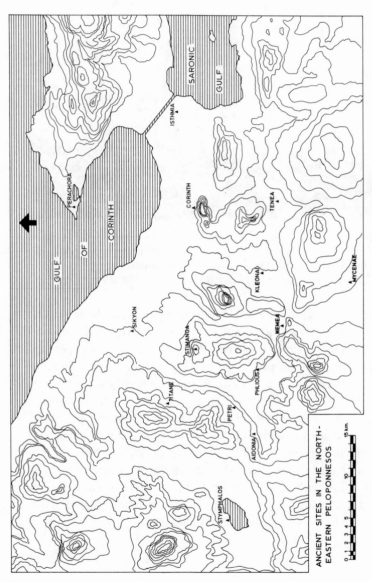

ANCIENT SITES IN THE NORTH-
EASTERN PELOPONNESOS

0 1 2 3 4 5   10   15 km.

Fig 1. Map showing the region of ancient Nemea.

Fig. 2. The Temple of Zeus from the northeast *ca.* 1805, with Mount Daouli in the background; the tumulus in the left background covers the Basilica, which was discovered in 1924; from W. Gell, *The Itinerary of Greece* (London 1810) Pl. 2.

tants, which, like Archaia Nemea, depends for the most part on Nea Nemea (and to a lesser extent on Argos) for its supplies and services. Modern inhabitants of the area (perhaps following ancient practice) go to Corinth only when bureaucratic necessities force a visit to the provincial capital.

The Nemea valley has been almost exclusively agricultural since the 1880s, when a team of French engineers opened the blocked gorge at the northern end, allowing the valley to drain and become arable. The village of Archaia Nemea dates from shortly thereafter. The peaceful atmosphere of the valley is broken occasionally by the noise of an unmuffled tractor or a chain saw and, somewhat less frequently these days, by the more venerable voice of a donkey.

II

HISTORY OF THE
EXCAVATIONS

Savants and scholars have always known Nemea, and a succession of early modern travelers visited the site. A collection of their impressions is in the foyer of the museum (see pp. 17–20). The earliest group of visitors was sponsored by the Society of the Dilettanti from London in 1766 (Fig. 3). According to the chronicler of that visit, the group excavated a small trench in front of the Temple of Zeus.[10] Apparently disappointed in their search for sculpture from the east pediment of the Temple, they soon abandoned the effort. Excavations were, indeed, discouraged by both the formidable quiet and the marshland created during the period of Turkish domination when the gorge north of the valley was blocked. An English visitor in 1805 noted: "The country around this place is remarkable for its humidity; and I believe that all the inhabitants, without a single exception, were afflicted with violent colds and coughs, as in England." He found Nemea "more characterised by gloom than most of the places I have seen. The splendour of religious pomp, and the busy animation of gymnastic and equestrian exercises, have been succeeded by the dreary vacancy of a death-like solitude."[11]

10. R. Chandler, *Travels in Greece* (Dublin 1766) 245.
11. E. Dodwell, *A Classical and Topographical Tour through Greece* II (London 1819) 209 and 210–11, respectively.

The situation changed when in 1883 a French engineering team drained the valley. The following year French archaeologists excavated at the Temple of Zeus and in a ruined chapel south of the Temple (on the site of the Early Christian Basilica).[12] The French undertook some further work in 1912,[13] but in neither campaign was much earth removed, and the site remained essentially unexplored.

In 1924 the French School ceded its rights to excavate at Nemea to the American School of Classical Studies at Athens, and excavations soon began under the sponsorship of the University of Cincinnati and the leadership of Bert Hodge Hill and Carl W. Blegen. These excavations took place in three successive annual campaigns, with some notable results.[14] The crypt at the western end of the Temple of Zeus, the long Altar east of the Temple, Oikos 1 (then called an enclosure), the Bath, and the western end of the Xenon (then called a *gymnasion*) were all discovered. The Basilica was recognized, and the location of the Stadium confirmed. Work on Tsoungiza recovered significant material of the early Neolithic age, and of the Early, Middle, and Late Bronze Age. During these campaigns an area of nearly three acres along the southern side of the Temple of Zeus was added to the archaeological zone.

After the campaign of 1926 Nemea received little attention until 1962. In that year Charles K. Williams undertook to produce the long-awaited publication of the Temple of Zeus and began clearing operations toward that end. In 1964 a full

12. G. Cousin and F. Dürrbach, "Inscriptions de Némée," *BCH* 9 (1885) 349–56.

13. Reported by M. Clemmensen and R. Vallois, "Le Temple de Zeus à Némée," *BCH* 49 (1925) 1–20.

14. C. W. Blegen, "The American Excavation at Nemea, Season of 1924," *Art and Archaeology* 19 (1925) 175–84, "The December Excavations at Nemea," *Art and Archaeology* 22 (1926) 127–34, 139, and "Excavations at Nemea, 1926," *AJA* 31 (1927) 421–40.

Fig. 3. The Temple of Zeus from the south in 1766, with Mount Apesas in the background; from *Antiquities of Ionia*, vol. 2 (London: Society of Dilettanti 1797) Pl. 15.

season of excavation took place.[15] Parts of Oikoi 2 and 3, the eastern part of the Xenon, and a part of the tile-kiln complex were uncovered. But after these discoveries, excavations ceased once again, and Nemea was left in comparative solitude for a decade.

In 1973 the University of California at Berkeley, under the aegis of the American School of Classical Studies at Athens, began its excavation project. That first year saw preliminary work, including a survey of the site and the establishment of a grid reference system, the purchase of property totaling some forty acres, the training of workers, the acquisition of tools, and so forth. From 1974 to 1986 the University of California continued a series of annual campaigns, the results of which will emerge in the following presentation.[16]

15. C. K. Williams, "Nemea," 'Αρχ. Δελτ. 20 (1965), Χρον. 154–56, BCH 89 (1965) 705–7, "Archaeology in Greece," JHS 85 (1965) 9, AJA 68 (1964) 201–2, AJA 69 (1965) 178–79.
16. See the annual reports in Hesperia listed in the Bibliography.

III

THE MUSEUM

Constructed as part of the excavation project of the University of California at Berkeley, thanks to the generosity of Mr. Rudolph A. Peterson, the archaeological museum of Ancient Nemea houses discoveries from the valley of Ancient Nemea as well as the valleys of Kleonai and Phlious, to the east and west, respectively.

It was dedicated and presented formally to the Greek state on May 28, 1984, and is operated by the Nauplion Ephoreia of the Archaeological Service of the Ministry of Culture. (See page i for its hours.)

The museum entrance is on the western side. The foyer opens on a courtyard (opposite the entrance) and on the main exhibition hall (at left), from which two large picture windows look out to the north over the Sanctuary of Zeus.

The Foyer

To the left of the entrance is the desk of the guardians of the museum (Fig. 4). On the wall in the southeastern corner are marble plaques on which are inscribed the names of both the donors to the Nemea project between 1973 and 1983 and the regular local workmen. A marble plaque on the wall at the entrance to the main exhibition hall honors the donor of the museum. To the left of that entrance, and partially behind the guardians' desk, are displayed one of the Corinthian capitals (A 20) and a drum from a Corinthian column (A 21) from the interior of the Temple of Zeus. These elements also appear in a restored drawing on the wall.

The display in the foyer consists of four three-sided islands on which are mounted engravings, photographs, and drawings that show in chronological sequence the early views of the valley and the Temple of Nemean Zeus. These materials illustrate a gradual but steady trend away from romantic points of view.

The first island, to the right of the entrance, displays on side a the work published by R. Chandler after a visit to Nemea in 1766. Side b has views by W. Gell (1805) and E. D. Clarke (1801), and side c shows photographs of original works by K. Haller von Hallerstein (1810) and W. Haygarth (1810).

The second island, nearer the courtyard, has engravings published by O. M. von Stackelberg (1813) and H. W. Williams (1817) on side a, drawings from A. Blouet (1829) on side b, and engravings from R. L. Letronne (*ca.* 1829) and C. Wordsworth (1832–1833) on side c.

To the left of the door to the courtyard is the third island, with the work of F. C. H. L. Pouqueville (1815–1818?) and E. Lear (1849) on side a. Side b displays engravings from R. R. Farrer (1880) and C. H. Hanson (1885?) and two early photographs from Nemea, by D. Baud-Bovy and F. Boissonnas (1908). On side c is a drawing of the Temple of Zeus begun by L. Lands (1936) and completed by C. K. Williams (1964).

The fourth island has more drawings by Lands and Williams on side a; on side b is an enlargement of an aerial photograph by W. and E. Myers that shows the condition of the Temple of Zeus in 1977 (Fig. 5). Side c displays drawings by F. A.

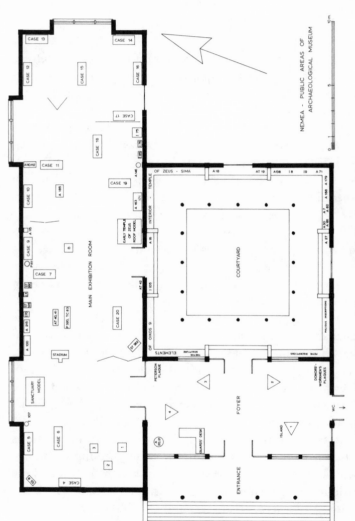

NEMEA - PUBLIC AREAS OF ARCHAEOLOGICAL MUSEUM

Fig. 4. Plan of the public areas and displays of the museum.

Cooper (1982), E. Stockton (1982), and M. Korres (1984) for
a partial reconstruction.

The Main Exhibition Hall

At the entrance to the main exhibition hall, three panels on
the right display photographs of the sites of Kleonai, Argos,
and (from the air in 1984) the Sanctuary of Zeus with the Stadium at the lower right.

KLEONAI was a city-state of secondary size and significance
located in the valley east of the Nemea valley (see p. 10). It has
never been excavated, although the remains of a small Temple
of Herakles of Hellenistic date are visible and evidence of
other monuments, such as a theater, is discernible on the surface. Nemea, never a city-state but rather a Panhellenic athletic and religious festival center, was originally controlled
and administered to by Kleonai (see nn. 35 and 38). According to ancient literary tradition,[17] the Nemean Games were
founded in 573 B.C. and were controlled by Kleonai as of
that date.

ARGOS, a major power in the ancient Greek world, is located about 23 km. south of Nemea by the modern road. In
the 5th century B.C. it expanded, swallowing other, smaller,
city-states such as Tiryns and Mycenae. By around 400 B.C.
Argos had gained control of the Nemean Games and of the
site itself (and, perhaps, of Kleonai as well), and thereafter the
games were more frequently held at Argos than at Nemea.
Visitors to the museum can follow the history of the shifts
between Argos and Nemea through the medium of the archaeological artifacts on display. Although the location of the
stadium for the games at Argos has not been excavated, the
contours of a stadium are recognizable in the ravine between
the Larissa and Aspis hills.

17. Hieronymous, *Chronicle* (ed. Fotheringham 1922) 179.

Fig. 5. Aerial view of the Temple of Zeus, 1977.

The topography in the AERIAL VIEW of the Sanctuary of Zeus and the Stadium in 1984 (Fig. 6) differs from the present (1988) topography in that the dirt road that once ran east–west through the sanctuary north of the museum was replaced by a bypass to the east in 1985.

To the left of the entrance, on the opposite wall, is a MAP of the eastern Mediterranean. The Panhellenic games at Nemea (like those at Olympia, Delphi, and Isthmia) attracted both competitors and visitors from this whole region. The map shows where they came from, according to ancient written sources or the evidence of coins found in the excavations. Surely other cities, however, provided visitors for whom we have no specific evidence.

Three cases in front of the map hold a sampling of the COINS, a few of which have been reproduced in photographs on the wall to the left. The display gives an idea of the range of geography and chronology represented by the coins. The heavy proportion of silver to bronze may be explained by the long-distance traveler's need for the more valuable silver coins, which were then left behind at Nemea, either out of carelessness or in the form of dedications.

CASE I: COINS FROM THE NEIGHBORHOOD

This display includes representative coins from the city-states near Nemea. It is not surprising that three of them—Corinth, Sikyon, and Argos—provided a large percentage of the more than four thousand coins found at Nemea. Nemea's closest neighbors, Kleonai and Phlious, are less well represented, at least in part because of limited issue and circulation. Then, too, Kleonai was incorporated into Argos for much of its history. (Samples of all the coin types in this case are shown in photographs on the wall.)

CASE 2: COINS FROM DISTANT VISITORS

Here are displayed representative coins from many Greek city-states. These include the heavy silver "turtles" of Aigina, issues of individual cities in Arkadia as well as of the Arkadian League, and the "owls" of Athens. Other city-states and regions represented are Eleusis, Megara, Boiotia, Thebes, Tanagra, Phokis, Opuntian Lokris, Chalkis, Histiaia, Lamia, Oita, Elis, Hermione, Epidauros, Messene, Tiryns, the Achaian League, and Sparta.

CASE 3: COINS OF HELLENISTIC AND LATER TIMES

This case contains three distinct collections. The first shows representative coins of Macedonian kings beginning with

Fig. 6.   Aerial view of the Sanctuary of Zeus and the Stadium, 1984.

Philip II and his son Alexander the Great. The games, long
absent from Nemea (see pp. 43 and 61–62), were returned
around 330 B.C., that is, just after the Macedonian victory
at Chaironeia in 338 B.C. Scholars generally agree that after
his victory there, Philip instituted a "Greek League of Nations." [18] The *synedrion,* "council," of this league was to meet
each year at the Panhellenic festival center that was celebrating the games (Olympia, Delphi, Isthmia, or Nemea). It
seems likely that the return of the games to Nemea at this
time was occasioned by the creation of the league and that the
concentration of Macedonian coins found in the excavations
reflects the influence exerted by those kings upon the site.

The second collection in case 3 is of Roman times and Roman emperors. Because the games moved permanently from

18. Scholars today call this league the League of Corinth, even though there
is no ancient evidence for such a name.

Nemea to Argos well before 100 B.C., Nemea received only casual visitors after this date. Thus few coins from Roman times have been found in the excavations; nearly all of them are on display here.

The third collection shows samples of Byzantine and Frankish coins from about A.D. 500 to 1300. Much evidence remains of a 6th-century Early Christian community which grew up among the ruins (see the account of case 10, p. 43). Not surprisingly, the Dark Ages which followed are poorly represented at Nemea, but there is great numismatic activity from the time of Emperor Manuel I (A.D. 1143–1180) through the Frankish invasions of the 13th century, including even English coins issued by Henry III from 1222 to 1237. The excavations have revealed, however, very few other signs of activity during that time, and it is uncertain whether these coins reflect a permanent community or some other activity.

CASE 4: THE MYTHS OF NEMEA

All ancient sites had their own myths, and the Panhellenic centers were no exception. The myths for Nemea are represented in the excavated material in case 4 on the west wall of the main exhibition hall. In Greek mythology, perhaps no hero is so enduring as Herakles, and his victory over the lion—the first of his twelve labors—clearly associates him with Nemea.[19] Because the skin of the lion was impenetrable, Herakles had to wrestle the lion and strangle him. Then, with the lion's own claws, Herakles skinned the beast, thereafter wearing the skin over his back as a kind of armor (Alexander

19. This myth was very popular and occurs frequently in art and literature. The earliest literary example is in Hesiod, *Theogony*, 327–32 (8th century B.C.). It is interesting that Hesiod himself, warned by the Pythian oracle that death would overtake him in the fair grove of Nemean Zeus, avoided Nemea (cf. Thucydides 3.96.1 and Plutarch, *Moralia* 162D). Unfortunately for Hesiod, there was also a grove of Nemean Zeus at Lokris.

the Great adopted this same iconographical device in his coins; see case 3, C 337). One reads in general handbooks and guides that Herakles, as a thanksgiving to his father Zeus for his victory over the lion, established the Sanctuary of Zeus and the games. The only archaeological evidence of the myth discovered at Nemea consists of small bronze lion's head attachments and a gold foil relief representation of Herakles' face with the lion's skin tied under his chin (BR 1040 and GJ 26; see the photographic enlargements on the wall behind case 4). The paucity of evidence is not surprising, however, for the connection between Herakles' victory over the lion and the founding of the Nemean Games was not mentioned in ancient literature until the 1st century after Christ.[20]

The proper foundation myth for the Nemean Games has to do with a set of characters less well known but established well before the 5th century B.C., when Aeschylus wrote a play about them, only the title of which survives. Of a later play by Euripides, *Hypsipyle*, perhaps a third has been preserved on a papyrus from Egypt, and that together with later texts gives us the following story.[21]

Once upon a time in Nemea there was either a priest of Zeus or a king named Lykourgos who, with his wife Eurydike, longed for an heir. After many years of frustration, a baby boy was born, and the happy couple gave him the name Opheltes. Lykourgos sent to Delphi to ask how he might ensure the health and happiness of his baby, and the Pythian

20. See Virgil, *Georgics* 3.19 with *scholium* (Servius-Probus) *ad loc.* Attempts to use the texts of Callimachus, *Victoria Berenices* (text in *ZPE* 14 [1977] 1–50), and Euphorion *apud* Plutarch, *Moralia* 677A (= Powell, *Collectanea Alexandrina* 84), to establish a cause-and-effect relation between the lion's death and the founding of the games are less than convincing. But even if such interpretations could be proved correct, the relation would still not be traced earlier than the 3rd century B.C.

21. For the sources and discussion of the myth, see E. Simon, "Archemoros," *AA* (1979) 31–45; and W. Pülhorn, "Archemoros," *LIMC* II (Zurich 1984) 472–75. Note that it was known already to Simonides of Keos, to Pindar, and to Bacchylides.

oracle responded that the baby was not to be allowed to touch the ground until he had learned to walk.

Upon his return to Nemea, Lykourgos acquired a slave woman named Hypsipyle,[22] to whom he entrusted the care of the baby Opheltes, with the stipulation that he was not to be allowed to touch the ground. One day Hypsipyle was carrying the baby in the valley when she was approached by the Seven Champions, who were on their way from Argos to Thebes. They asked Hypsipyle for something to drink, and she led them to a spring or stream where she laid the baby down on a bed of wild celery (σέλινον) to fetch water for them. While her back was turned, a serpent killed the baby. The Seven took this death as a bad omen for their own expedition (correctly, as it turned out); they renamed the baby Archemoros, "beginner of doom." In an attempt to propitiate the gods, they held funeral games, thus founding the Nemean Games, with judges (Hellanodikai) clothed in black robes as a sign of mourning and a crown of wild celery as the symbol of victory. Among the few depictions of this myth is that on a sarcophagus of Roman date in the Corinth museum,[23] shown here in a photograph on the wall.

Given this mythical background for the Nemean Games, it would not be surprising to find relevant physical evidence. Indeed, a small bronze figurine in case 4 (Fig. 7) must represent Opheltes; the pose of the figurine is similar to that of Opheltes on the Corinthian sarcophagus. Although the figurine belongs to the Hellenistic period, it was found south of

22. This Hypsipyle has a history of her own. The daughter of King Thoas of Lemnos, she ruled the island and received the Argonauts on their (not always very energetic) quest for the Golden Fleece. She had two sons, Euneos and Thoas, by Jason, but after Jason's departure she was captured by pirates and sold to Lykourgos of Nemea. In the Euripidean version of the story she is rescued from Nemea by her two sons after a miraculous recognition; see Euripides, *Hypsipyle* (ed. Bond) 16–18 and 147–49.

23. F. P. Johnson, *Corinth* IX, *Sculpture, 1896–1923* (Cambridge, Mass. 1931) 114–19, no. 241. For more recent photographs, see Simon, *op. cit.* (n. 21) 40–41, Figs. 7–9.

Fig. 7. Bronze baby Opheltes (BR 671).

the Temple of Zeus in earth disturbed in the 6th century after Christ. Its archaeological significance is therefore limited.

Much clearer is the evidence of the hero shrine, or Heroön, discovered southwest of the Temple and west of the Bath (no. 19 in the model; see pp. 34, 104–10). An aerial photograph (see Fig. 36) of this Heroön near case 4 shows it as a lopsided pentagon built of rectangular blocks overlying a curvilinear predecessor built of field stones (this structure is clearest at the lower left, or southwestern, corner of the photograph). The religious character of the Heroön was established by, among other evidence, the deliberate burial of a krater (P 539 in case 4) with a stone lid at the northeastern corner of the enclosure, next to the foundations. A photograph on the wall shows this krater at the moment of discovery. Its contents

may have included the beans which were set in such foundation trenches when a structure was dedicated to the gods.[24]

Within the enclosure were deposits of ash, carbon, and
burnt bone from sacrifices and large quantities of other artifacts; another wall photograph shows some of this material
during excavation. Everything in case 4, with the exception
of the lion's head (BR 1040), the gold foil Herakles (GJ 26), and
the figurine of Opheltes (BR 671), came from this enclosure.
The miniature vessels are characteristic of the votives one
might expect in a shrine, and the drinking cups (e.g., P 510)
were used for libations poured out during sacrificial rites. The
fragment of a terracotta column (AT 83) once supported a
basin for holy water (*perirrhanterion*), the rim of which may
well have been inscribed with a sadly fragmentary dedication
(P 547, a–f). The cup-skyphos (P 546), which bears an inscribed dedication by a victor as well as a magical inscription,
also shows the decidedly religious character of this enclosure.
The silver coins of Sikyon (C 1639) and Aigina (C 1645 and
1649) would also have been appropriate dedications in a shrine.

Even more suggestive, however, is the iron caduceus (IL
324), the symbol of Hermes Psychopompos, leader of souls
to the underworld. It hints that the shrine is chthonic and he-
roic. The same conclusion derives from the lead curse tablets,
two of which are displayed in case 4 (IL 327 and 367). Such
curses are appropriately deposited in the shrine of a hero. The
examples in case 4 bear erotic curses in which an anonymous
author hopes to alienate the affections of a woman from another man. Thus IL 327 reads: "I am turning Euboula away
from Aineas, away from his face, from his eyes, from his
mouth, from his breast, from his soul, from his stomach,
from his penis, from his anus, from his whole body am I
turning Euboula away from Aineas."

24. See Aristophanes, *Plutus* 1198 and *Pax* 923, and *scholia ad loc*. I thank C.
Simon for this reference. See further p. 107, on the Heroön.

Fig. 8. Terracotta baby Opheltes (TC 117).

To which hero was the shrine at Nemea dedicated? Pausanias, who visited Nemea in the mid-2nd century after Christ,
found there a tomb of Opheltes within a peribolos which also
contained altars. He defined the peribolos as an enclosure of
stone (ϑριγκὸς λίϑων) in the same words he used to describe
the peribolos enclosing the Tomb of Pelops at Olympia (see
p. 110 and n. 61). The enclosure at Nemea seems to satisfy the
architectural requirements of the peribolos surrounding the
Tomb of Opheltes. Two figurines discovered within the enclosure provide further evidence. One is a badly worn stone
statuette of a woman holding a child to her bosom (ss 3, in a
photograph on the wall); the other is a terracotta of a seated
baby boy apparently holding a mask to his face, a gesture of
chthonic significance (Fig. 8). We may be reasonably con-
fident, then, that the Heroön is concerned with the Tomb of
Opheltes.

To the right of case 4, in the northwestern corner of the room, is the right half of a MARBLE RELIEF (ss 8), part of a dedicatory relief which had been reused in a house of the later 4th century B.C. (see p. 76 and Fig. 23). It portrays a male figure standing in front of a seated female. The figures have yet to be identified, and the date is in debate, although it is probably in the 460s B.C. Clearly the piece must stand early in the Classical period since it combines elements of the Classical, especially in the male figure, with elements of the earlier, Archaic, period, especially in the female figure. The male's clothing, for example, is plastic, the female's stiff and two-dimensional. The handling of depth is awkward both with regard to the female's feet and in the relation of her breast to her shoulder.

CASES 5 AND 6: RELIGIOUS DEDICATIONS

The artifacts from various votive deposits displayed here reveal many characteristics of worship in the Sanctuary of Zeus. On the top shelf, left, of case 5 are artifacts from a votive deposit consisting of an informal pit with ashes from a sacrifice (see the photograph on the wall beside the case). In this pit were some small terracotta toys or animals (M 1 and TC 1) and several dozen miniature vases (P 2–44). It would appear that credit went more to the quantity than the size of the vessels dedicated. The only larger piece of pottery gives us the name of the dedicator, Aischylion, which is scratched on the bottom of a skyphos (P 1).

The top shelf, right, displays material from a ritual meal pyre. The vessels, of normal size, include utilitarian items such as lamps (L 187 and 189). The meal appears to have ended with the smashing of the drinking cups, perhaps by means of the rocks discovered in them. On the wall one can see the skyphos (P 1338) still in the ashes of the pyre with the stone (ST 651) inside it.

The bottom shelf of case 5 represents yet another type of votive deposit. On the slopes of the valley's eastern side, several hundred meters from the Temple of Zeus, a simple pit was discovered cut into the soft natural bedrock. Roughly circular, about 2 m. in diameter and 1 m. deep, this pit contained some 526 vases. Many were nestled inside one another and neatly stacked, and the pit cannot, therefore, represent a garbage dump. Different shapes were represented in rich abundance: the kylix (P 1022), skyphos (P 951), lamp (L 164), miniature hydria (P 1057), and kalathos (P 1004). Although the dates of the vessels range over at least two generations, all were buried together about 480 B.C. They may reflect an attempt to hide votive offerings of the Sanctuary of Zeus or some other shrine, for there is no clear evidence of the deity to whom they had been dedicated.

Case 6 contains other types of dedications made in the Sanctuary of Zeus. The silver coins on the circular stand were found in a deposit of ash and burnt bone from sacrificial debris. Although the circumstances of their discovery indicate that they were consecrated to Zeus, it is not clear whether they were deposited by a single person, for their geographical range is fairly large: Sikyon (C 901, 902, 904), Athens (C 903), Aigina (C 905), Phlious (C 906), and Corinth (C 1659). To the left of the coins is material from the destruction debris of the Early Temple of Zeus (see case 19, p. 60). Each fragment must represent part of the wealth of the sanctuary in the early 5th century B.C. This wealth includes a miniature double ax (IL 376), the head of a young man (BR 897), attachments from vessels or furniture in the form of lions' heads (BR 849, 896, 898), a votive plaque with the incised figure of a bull (BR 708), and (toward the center of the case) a lead kouros, or young man (Fig. 9), made from a mold. Another kouros, from Isthmia, was made from the same mold—an indication of direct commerce between the Panhellenic sanctuaries.

Fig. 9. Lead kouros (IL 201).

Little has survived of the statues of victorious athletes—
another type of dedication common at Nemea. The olive
leaves which once made up the crowns on such statues (BR 74,
109, 139, etc.) and scraps of bronze statuary which can be recognized as hair (BR 999), feathers (BR 1000), or an eyelid
(BR 990) bear mute witness to the devastation the site has
endured. Smaller dedications were less attractive to vandals
and thus remain to the archaeologist. These include terracotta
figurines of horses and riders (TC 38, 90, 131, 136, etc.), of a
Persian warrior (TC 91), of the god Pan (TC 95), and of Zeus
himself (TC 69). So too miniature vases like those already seen
in other contexts abound (P 54 and 55, 333 and 334, etc.), as
do *aryballoi,* the flasks in which ancient athletes carried the oil
with which they coated their bodies before exercise (P 97,
239, 559). In addition to such artifacts known to have belonged to Zeus because they were discovered in sacrificial
contexts, other, more prosaic, items are specifically labeled
as his property. One example is the mug incised τοῦ Διός,
"property of Zeus" (P 778; see p. 76).

On the wall between case 5 and the picture window is a PHOTOGRAPH of the open square which surrounded the Temple of Zeus. Excavations here revealed the pits which once contained the cypress trees of the Sacred Grove (*alsos* in Greek; see pp. 157–59 and Fig. 58). The cypress, sometimes associated with mourning, would have been especially appropriate to a sanctuary associated with the death of the baby Opheltes.

A STONE PILLAR next to these photographs has thirteen vertical facets above a rough "base" which was originally inserted into the ground (I 107). Near the top of the pillar is the inscription ΩΡΟΣ ΕΠΙΠΟΛΑΣ, "Boundary of the Flat Area," in Argive letters of the late 4th century B.C. It would seem, then, that the Sacred Square at Nemea was officially called the Epipola just as Olympia had its Altis and Delphi its Peribolos.

MODEL

In front of the picture window is a model, on a scale of 1:200, of the Sanctuary of Zeus as it would have appeared in about 300 B.C. It is the work of Robert Garbish (compare the plan of the sanctuary, Fig. 10). The flat open squares represent areas not yet excavated. Buildings numbered 1–8 represent the first 8 *oikoi* (see p. 118 for the various meanings of this word) erected by various city-states for the use of their citizens and guests at Nemea (see pp. 62–63, 67–71, 117–27, 160–68). Numbers 9 and 10 are the Temple and Altar of Zeus, respectively, whereas 11 and 13 represent buildings the precise nature of which has not been established. Number 12 refers to the Epipola with its Sacred Grove of cypress trees and other altars and monuments. The Dining Establishment (14) is attached to some of the *oikoi* but also clearly differs from them. The number 15 marks an area of light industry (see case 20, p. 63) and a series of wells (see case 9, p. 39). The hotel, or Xenon, is 16 and the Bath 17. The Nemea River is marked 18, and to the west of it

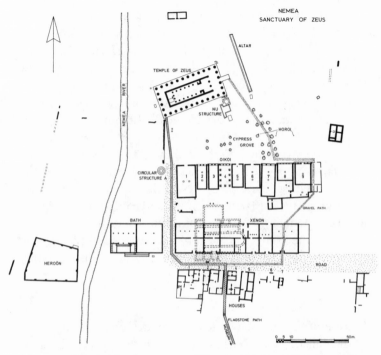

Fig. 10. Plan of the Sanctuary of Zeus with the walk indicated.

is the hero shrine, or Heroön (19). The region labeled 20 contains a number of houses, probably for the priests or the judges of the Nemean Games.

In the view from the window, the houses (20) are in the immediate foreground, just beyond the edge of the grass. The highest and most massive remains beyond them, consisting largely of gray stones, are of the Early Christian Basilica which lies over the Xenon (16). To the right, or east, of the Basilica the wall of the Xenon comes out from under the church and continues eastward. Finally, the columns of the Temple of Zeus (9) are clearly visible in the background.

Near the model of the sanctuary is a MODEL OF THE STA-DIUM. Its orientation to and distance from the sanctuary are proportionally correct, although it is in fact higher in elevation. Indeed, the side of the Evangelistria Hill into which the Stadium was built is visible from the sanctuary model through the window above and behind the Stadium model.

On the wall to the right of the picture window are two groups of color representations of the various events in the ancient games. These have already been described (pp. 4–5).

Below them is a STARTING BLOCK with a single groove for the toes of the runner (A 100). It was probably used originally in the early stadium of the 6th century B.C., which has not yet been discovered, although it must have been near the Temple of Zeus.[25] As can be seen in the photograph on the wall above, the block was reused as a threshold in a door of the Xenon (cf. p. 169). Beside this starting block is a BLOCK OF HARD GRAY LIMESTONE on the upper surface of which is carved a small groove for a single foot (A 215). Like similarly grooved blocks found in Corinth, this one is from a starting line. A vertical socket at one end of it received a post marking the division of lanes; a *lambda* (Λ) inscribed in front of the socket marks this as the twelfth lane. This block cannot be from the Stadium and so might be from some other race course, perhaps that of the *gymnasion*. Two more of these blocks are in the foundations of an Early Christian basilica on the crest of Evangelistria Hill.

On the north wall above and to the right is an AERIAL PHOTOGRAPH of the Stadium as it appeared in 1980 (see Fig. 61), with the main features—starting line, water channel, judges' stand, and tunnel entrance—marked out.

On the CENTER ISLAND opposite the aerial photograph of the Stadium is a pair of the terracotta water pipes which brought fresh drinking water into the Stadium (TC 40 and 41). The joints of these pipes, which date from the late 4th century B.C., were originally sealed with a white clay mortar, in-

25. See D. G. Romano, "The Early Stadium at Nemea," *Hesperia* 46 (1977) 27–31.

dicating that water may have come into the Stadium under pressure. Two photographs on the panel above the pipes show them in the Stadium during their excavation.

The other (southern) side of the center island exhibits two terracotta water channels (TC 107 and 83) and an amphora (P 320) which was reused in the entrance passageway to the Stadium as a settling basin, as can be seen in the photograph on the panel above. Water ran into the amphora through "windows" cut in its sides, allowing dirt and debris to settle out before the water continued its journey. This channel is discussed further on page 175. Also on the panel above are detailed photographs of two artifacts in case 7: a bronze *strigil* (BR 857), with which an athlete scraped off the sweat, oil, and dirt at the end of his exercise, and a dedicatory plaque (BR 1098).

Further on along the NORTH WALL of the exhibition hall is a fragment of stone from a voussoir of the Stadium tunnel and, in the photograph above, the same stone at the time of discovery, fallen on the floor of the tunnel (I 70). This stone, like so many still in place in the tunnel, bears a scratched graffito. Now incomplete, it originally gave the name of an athlete with the adjective *kalos,* "beautiful."

A photograph on the wall to the right of I 70 shows the tunnel during excavation. Although the two ends had silted shut, a considerable open space in the center was used as a refuge in the 6th century after Christ (cf. pp. 47, 188–90).

The next photographs show other graffiti in the tunnel. One, I 59, has the verb NIKΩ, "I win," followed, in a different hand, by the name Telestas. This is probably the Telestas who won the boxing event at Olympia in the boys' category in around 340 B.C.[26]

---

26. Pausanias 6.14.4. The date of Telestas's victory is not absolutely precise and depends on the career of Silanion, the sculptor of Telestas's statue at Olympia; cf. L. Moretti, *Olympionikai. I vincitori negli antichi agoni Olimpici* (*Atti della Accademia Nazionale dei Lincei, Memorie,* ser. 8, vol. 8, Rome 1957) no. 453.

Fig. 11. Aristis stele (I 4).

The other graffito, I 63 (see Fig. 66), has ΑΚΡΟΤΑΤΟΣ
ΚΑΛΟΣ, "Akrotatos is beautiful," followed, in a different
hand, by ΤΟΥ ΓΡΑΨΑΝΤΟΣ, "to the one who wrote it."
Akrotatos is almost certainly the Spartan prince who was
king from about 265 to 252 B.C., well known for his physical
beauty and his penchant for "Persian luxuries."[27]

At the base of the wall below the photographs just mentioned are TWO BLACK MARBLE STATUE BASES from the Stadium. ST 126 preserves the outline of a left foot, which would
have been leaded in place. ST 260 preserves the lead which
held its statue in place: the statue had two projections from
the sole of each foot rather than the outline of the foot itself.
Given the location of these bases near the starting line of the

27. Plutarch, *Agis* 3.4 and *Pyrrhus* 26.8, 28.2–3; Pausanias 3.6.6; Phylarchus
apud Athenaeus 4.142b. The precise grammatical significance of this graffito has
generated considerable interest; see Bibliography, p. 202.

Stadium, they may well have held statues of victorious athletes and should be dated to around 300 B.C..

Between the two black marble bases stands a relatively tall LIMESTONE PILLAR (I 4), the top of which has two square cuttings, each with smaller sockets within (the right one still has some lead in place). These would have held a statue, but one of a much earlier date than those mentioned in the preceding paragraph. On the face of the pillar (Fig. 11) is a very early Greek inscription with curious letter forms whose lines read alternately from left to right and right to left. (This style of writing, from a time when the Greek language had not yet settled into a standard written form, is called *boustrophedon*, from the turning of the oxen at the end of each plowed furrow in a field.) The stone speaks: "Aristis dedicated me to Zeus, the son of Kronos, the king having won the *pankration* four times at Nemea. (Aristis) the son of Pheidon of Kleonai." The forms of the letters indicate that it was around 550 B.C. that this local boy did very well in the Nemean Games over a period of at least six years.[28]

CASE 7: ATHLETIC EQUIPMENT

This case is devoted to athletic gear. In the left (northern) end is material found east of the Temple of Zeus in a single pit, as can be seen in a photograph on the north wall. It includes an iron discus (IL 419) weighing about 8.5 kg., as opposed to a typical weight of 2–3 kg. for the more usual stone or bronze discuses; a jumping weight, or *halter*, of lead (IL 418); javelin points (IL 420 and 435); iron spits, called *obeloi* (IL 421 and 424); drinking cups, or skyphoi (P 867–870); and a miniature oinochoe (P 866). This deposit would seem to represent a party following the (successful?) conclusion of a competition

28. D. W. Bradeen, "Inscriptions from Nemea," *Hesperia* 35 (1966) 320–23; cf. L. H. Jeffery, *The Local Scripts of Archaic Greece* (Oxford 1961) 148 and 150, no. 5.

in the pentathlon, after which both athletic and drinking gear were dedicated to Zeus.

In addition to the bases of the bronze statues which once graced the Stadium, dozens of fragments of those statues have been discovered. They include fragments of hair (BR 474, 477, 596, 553, 602), eyelids (BR 475 and 483), wrist (BR 467), and hip (BR 417). Athletic gear includes a fragment of a jumping weight, or *halter,* of stone (ST 626); bronze *strigils* (BR 729 and 857), one with the stamp of a horse and rider shown enlarged in a photograph on the central island; and an *aryballos* (P 436). From the equestrian events come an iron bit (IL 386); a number of gearlike spools from "snaffle bits," designed to prevent the horse from taking the bit in his teeth (BR 357, 457, 544, 940); and a bronze plaque which must once have been attached to the statue of a horse dedicated by its victorious owner (BR 1098; photograph on central island). The forms of the letters on the plaque indicate that it came from the city-state of Sikyon around 500 B.C. The plaque says that the statue of a horse was dedicated to Zeus.

CASE 9: WELLS AND THEIR CONTENTS

Nemea is a difficult and frustrating site to excavate. Unlike city-states with continual habitation and a fairly uniform buildup of layers of construction or destruction or habitation debris, Nemea was occupied only once every two years for a few days or weeks at the most. In the meantime the weeds grew up, and with the advent of the games it was necessary to chop them down (thus retaining the same basic ground level), whitewash the buildings, and generally clean up. Since such activities inevitably destroyed the layers on which archaeologists depend, the wells which were not so easily cleaned up are particularly important to our understanding of the history of Nemea. The results of the excavation of two wells are pre-

sented here, both in the region between the *oikoi* and the
Xenon (15 on the model).

As can be seen in the photographs on the panel to the right
of case 9, the excavation of a well is tricky and potentially
dangerous. Once the fill has been removed to a depth of
roughly 2 m., a means must be set up to pull out the excavated earth and to lower and raise the well digger. For these
purposes excavators at Nemea use the time-honored wind-
lass, once standard equipment for every village house. The
rubble walls of the well must be examined constantly and
consolidated from time to time. The greatest difficulty comes
at the depth of the water table, where a pump must work
alongside the digger. At that point a safety line for the digger,
a line from which the pump is suspended, the cord providing
power to the pump, the hose bringing the water out of the
well, and the line with which the excavated mud and antiquities are removed must enter the mouth of the well together.
The digger must be willing to endure cramped, dark, wet,
cold quarters. The information retrieved, however, justifies
the effort.

The bottom shelf of case 9 displays some of the discoveries
from a well designated L 17:1, a cross-sectional drawing
of which is on the wall left of the case. This drawing shows
that relatively few artifacts lay in the upper several meters of
closing fill, but among them were the inscription (I 104) from
which we learn that in 311 B.C. Demetrios Poliorketes, one of
the successors of Alexander the Great, established a league,
probably modeled on that of Philip (see the discussion of case
3, p. 23), which was to meet at Nemea.[29] Not until the excavation reached a depth of more than 8.50 m. from the ancient ground surface was a level of use encountered in the
well. Such levels are characterized by drinking cups and especially by larger vessels which were lowered down the well to
fetch water but broke and remained there whole or, more fre-

29. D. J. Geagan, "Inscriptions from Nemea," *Hesperia* 37 (1968) 381–84.

Fig. 12. Kore head on handle of bronze hydria (BR 379).

quently, in parts. This level of use produced, among other items, the large amphora (P 411) which stands to the left of case 9, a saltcellar (P 282), and a spouted jug (P 412).

Below this level of use came a destruction/cleanup level, as is most clear from the terracotta sima, or roof gutter, with a corner lion's head waterspout for directing rain water away from the building it adorned (AT 55). This piece is of considerable intrinsic architectural interest (a plug on its bottom surface is visible in the photograph on the panel to the right); it also tells us that a building at Nemea was damaged or destroyed and its elements thrown away. The same must be true of the building to which belonged the monolithic limestone column with a high square base (A 115), also found in the destruction/cleanup fill; the column now rests to the right of case 9. The cleanup occurred near the end of the 5th century B.C.; from it the drinking cups also come (P 290 and 291) and perhaps the bases for bronze vessels (BR 378, 380, 381).

The most notable discovery at this level of the well was the bronze hydria (Fig. 12) displayed in CASE 8, with photographs on the panel to the right. The female head on its handle allows us to date it originally to the late 6th century B.C., while the later inscription on its rim ("I belong to Zeus at Nemea") makes it clearly a possession of the sanctuary.

Below this level came a level of use which produced such pottery as a skyphos (P 278), a ribbed lekythos (P 292), and an oinochoe (P 276), all from the second half of the 5th century B.C. Below this the well ended at a depth of 9.95 m.

The top shelf of case 9 presents material from another well, located fairly close to the one represented on the bottom shelf. The second well, labeled L 17:2, was located immediately north of the baptistry of the Early Christian Basilica. Unlike its neighbor, L 17:2 either remained open in its upper levels or was cleaned out in the 5th or 6th century after Christ, for it was used as the ultimate destination of water drained from the baptismal font. A level of use was encountered about 7.50 m. below the mouth of the well (see the cross-sectional drawing on the panel to the right) which produced material of the second half of the 4th century B.C., including an amphora (P 400) and a mug (P 399). Immediately below this level came one of destruction/cleanup which produced a terracotta sima (AT 75) from the same unknown building as the example in L 17:1. Other material, such as the amphora handles stamped with a palmette (P 401 a–b), establishes a date late in the 5th century B.C. for this level. Immediately below came another level of use, from the second half of the 5th century, with material such as the lamp (L 45) and a skyphos (P 397). Below this the well ended.

These two wells reveal a strikingly similar history. Both were constructed in the second half of the 5th century and were used for a relatively brief period; near the end of the same century both were filled with the debris of a destruction or a cleanup following a destruction. Then for more than half a century—until the last three decades of the 4th century— neither well shows evidence of any activity. Before long, both wells were closed and put out of use. These data are significant because they suggest that for more than the first half of the 4th century B.C. the Sanctuary of Zeus at Nemea was not being used; that is, the Nemean Games were not at Nemea during that period.[30] The suggestion is reinforced, moreover, by the lack of artifacts of the first half of the 4th century over the whole of the sanctuary. Virtually none of the coins or the pottery, for example, can be dated to that period. A picture thus emerges of a destruction (see further at case 19, p. 61) in the late 5th century B.C., followed by some two generations of silence and desolation at the Panhellenic center of Nemean Zeus.

The PANELS TO THE LEFT OF CASE 10 take us to the later history of Nemea. At the upper left is an aerial view of the Early Christian Basilica (see Fig. 25), which dates from the 5th or, more likely, early 6th century after Christ. This church, the centerpiece of a settlement which grew up among the ruins of the old Panhellenic sanctuary, is the most prominent monument of that time in the area, although the basilica on the crest of the Evangelistria Hill is of similar date (see p. 80 and n. 46). At the lower left of this panel a photograph shows a detail of the baptistry, with its tile paving, and the sunken font from which came the larger fragment (mended from four joining pieces) of the marble ritual dining table displayed on the center island (A 185).[31] It had been reused, upside down, as the paving of the font, as can be seen in the photograph on the southern side of the center island. Another

30. That Nemean Games did take place, albeit not at Nemea, is shown by a number of references, including those to the victories of athletes such as Damiskos of Messene, Eupolemos of Elis, Hegesarchos of Arkadia, Sostratos of Sikyon (Pausanias 6.2.9, 6.3.7, 6.12.8, and 6.4.1–3, respectively) among many others during this period.

31. For similar tables and their probable purpose in the ritual feast called the agape, see G. Roux, "Tables Chrétiennes en marbre découvertes à Salamine," *Salamine de Chypre* IV (Paris 1973) 169–74; and J. Marcadé and G. Roux, "Tables et plateaux chrétiens en marbre découverts à Delphes," *Etudes delphiques* (*BCH* suppl. 4: Paris 1977) 455–57.

piece, probably from the same table, was found in the house attached to the southwestern corner of the Basilica. On the bottom surface of that piece is a ligature (shown in a photograph on the western side of the island) which might be interpreted as reading ΝΕΟΦΥΤΟΥ, "belonging to the born-again."

At the top of the panel closer to case 10 is a photograph of a typical area within the Sanctuary of Zeus. It is filled with relatively long and narrow trenches created in the Early Christian period for agricultural purposes. The vegetable gardens of modern Greece offer a precise analogy, but the more ancient version was responsible for considerable destruction of the site at Nemea. Below this photograph is another, showing the rubble walls of a large house built at the southwestern corner of the Basilica (cf. Figs. 28 and 29). It is clearly an architectural dependency of the church, a kind of rectory or parsonage.

CASE 10: ROMAN AND MEDIEVAL POTTERY

The top shelf, left, displays pottery from the Stadium tunnel, apparently used by people seeking shelter during the first two decades of the 1st century after Christ, before the water channel was put through (see p. 36). The deposit included a plate of the so-called Pergamene ware (P 365), two-handled mugs (P 467–469), a bowl (P 466), and lamps (L 36 and 38).

The top shelf, right, contains material from a well near the Temple of Zeus (K 14:3 just north of K 14:4 in case 18; see the photograph there), including bowls (P 345 and 346); a bronze bucket, or situla (BR 587); and lamps which show a bust of Athena (L 42) and the infant Herakles (L 41). This deposit from the late 3rd or early 4th century after Christ offers the only substantial evidence of activity at Nemea after the 2nd century B.C. and before the Early Christian settlement. It would appear that at this time activity was isolated at this well, which was cleaned out and deepened (cf. p. 128).

The bottom shelf, left, of case 10 presents typical pottery of the Early Christian period at Nemea (5th and 6th centuries after Christ). Particularly characteristic are the jugs (P 279 and 545) and the lamps, including L 125 with its cross in the top disc.

On the bottom shelf, right, are typical examples of Byzantine pottery of the 12th and 13th centuries, among them a glazed oinochoe (P 1192), a small glazed bowl with a sgraffito animal (P 164), and a handle stamped with the eagle of Constantinople (P 1238).

Black and white photographs on the WALL TO THE RIGHT OF CASE 10 show a typical Early Christian cemetery before and after the graves were excavated. This cemetery was located just south of the Temple of Zeus, but others have been found at the northwestern corner of the Temple, midway between it and the Bath, and especially around the Basilica.

The three small marble columns (A 110–112) on the LOW BASE near the picture window may have been part of the iconostasis of the Basilica.

CASE 11: THE EARLY CHRISTIANS

Several artifacts here reveal details about the life of the Early Christian community at Nemea. At left is material from grave 7 in the cemetery at the northwestern corner of the Temple of Zeus. The two color photographs on the wall to the left show that this simple, typical grave was formed by setting roof tiles on edge along the sides and leaning them together at the top. Within the grave was the skeleton, together with more gifts than are typical (Fig. 13), including a bronze pin (GJ 49); a pair of ear spoons (BR 828 and 829), behind the head in the photograph; a pair of cosmetic spatulas (BR 830 and 856); a stone cosmetic palette (ST 518) found on the breast of the deceased; and a silver-plated bronze finger ring with an enigmatic monogram (GJ 66) which had stained the bone of the ring finger. The grave is clearly that of a relatively

Fig. 13. Grave 7 during excavation.

wealthy woman. Analysis of the skeletal remains indicates that she was young—about seventeen years—and suffered from anemia, a common ailment among the inhabitants of the settlement.

The center of case 11 has various personal effects from many other graves: finger rings (GJ 90, 1, 96, etc.), belt buckles (BR 721, 832, etc.), and crosses which could, in some cases, be folded up and concealed (GJ 84 and 85). The medallion of St. George and the dragon (BR 38) comes from the later Byzantine period. Glass goblets were common in the Early Christian settlement, but they were so thin that only their bases have survived (GL 24–27, etc.). The floor of the church (see the photograph of the baptistry on the panel to the left of case 10) was paved with baked tiles. One example in case 11 (AT 73) was marked by the manufacturer, who stuck his fingers into the wet clay. Early Christian trademarks were not complicated. The square bronze rod (BR 988) is actually calibrated with marks; it was the beam of a steelyard, or weighing scale, similar to the modern example in the photograph on the eastern side of the CENTER ISLAND.

The right (southern) side of case 11 is concerned with the end of the Early Christian settlement. This story, repeated throughout the Nemea valley, can be told succinctly from the discovery of animal bones, cooking pots (such as P 368), and a hoard of bronze coins (C 1509–1531, 1246) inside the entrance tunnel of the Stadium. At a date in the 580s after Christ, the tunnel, which had been silted shut at its ends but had a clear space some four feet high within, was entered after the removal of two voussoir blocks from its eastern end. A person or persons lived there for some little time (several days at least, to judge from the quantity of animal bones), and it must have been then that the graffito shown in the photograph on the wall was scratched: ΑΙΘΕΡΙΖΩΗΣ, "ethereal life," seems an appropriate sentiment for an Early Christian. The owner of the coins, which range from the time of Justinian I (C 1510 from A.D. 539/40) to that of Justin II (C 1523 from A.D. 576/7), did not return to claim them, falling victim, with the whole settlement, to the violent invasion of Slavic tribes at a date established from other parts of the excavations as no earlier than about A.D. 582. There was no recovery. For ages thereafter the archaeological picture at Nemea is very dark.

The EASTERN END OF THE MAIN EXHIBITION HALL is now devoted to the display of prehistoric artifacts. In due course these will be moved into the east wing and more material from the Sanctuary of Zeus displayed here. For the moment, however, the prehistory of the region is in this part of the museum.

Near the picture window is a pair of PANELS, the northern one of which shows a general view of the Nemea valley from

the east. West of the Sanctuary of Zeus the long, low hill
called Tsoungiza can be seen, running from north to south
like a spine through the valley. From the picture window the
northern end of this hill (which has no antiquities) can be seen
to the extreme left (west). Although scattered traces of prehistoric remains have been discovered in other parts of the
valley, including the Sanctuary of Zeus, concentrated prehistoric remains have been found exclusively on this hill.
(The configuration of the valley is such that Tsoungiza offers
a direct view of the citadel of Mycenae some 11 km. to the
southeast.)[32]

CASE 12: NEOLITHIC AND MYCENAEAN POTTERY

The top shelf displays a collection of pottery from an Early
Neolithic (6000–5000 B.C.) pit, probably a refuse dump,
from Tsoungiza. Even though no architectural remains of the
settlement of this period have been recovered on Tsoungiza,
the quantity of pottery, of which this is a very small sample,
shows that there was habitation of considerable size and duration. The two most characteristic pottery types from this period are those known as black ware, which has a highly polished black or dark gray surface (e.g., P 916, 930, 915, etc.),
and rainbow or variegated ware, which tends to have pink or
buff or orange at the top, gradually darkening through gray
to black at the bottom, both outside and in (e.g., P 929, 79,
etc.). The most common shape is the deep bowl, usually with

32. Excavations on the Tsoungiza ridge were first carried out in 1925 and
1926; cf. C. W. Blegen, *AJA* 31 (1927) 436–39; J. P. Harland, "The Excavations
of Tsoungiza, the Prehistoric Site of Nemea," *AJA* 32 (1928) 63; and C. W.
Blegen[†], "Neolithic Remains at Nemea," *Hesperia* 44 (1975) 251–79. The University of California at Berkeley next excavated there in 1974, 1975, 1979, and
1981; see appropriate annual reports in *Hesperia* and J. C. Wright, "Excavations
at Tsoungiza (Archaia Nemea), 1981," *Hesperia* 51 (1982) 375–97. At the invita-
tion of the University of California, Bryn Mawr College excavated on the hill
from 1984 to 1986. The material from these latest excavations remains to be
added to the museum exhibition.

Fig. 14. Vessels from house on Tsoungiza (P 685, 723, 724, 740, 708, 716, 722).

a ring base or foot, although some have rounded or nearly pointed bottoms. The least common shape is the askoid jug (P 920) with a rounded bottom and an ovoid body painted with red parallel zigzag lines. The large fragment of a collar-necked jar (P 931) is unusual for its decoration: the lower part was painted solid red while the upper part of the body bears two rows of elongated triangles painted in the same red.

With such examples from the thousands of vessels recovered from Early Neolithic deposits on Tsoungiza it becomes clear that this early phase of human activity in the Nemea valley was rich and lively.

On the bottom shelf, left, of case 12 are several vessels from the floor deposit of a house on Tsoungiza (Fig. 14). To the left of the case is a photograph of that house with many of the vessels still in place at the time of excavation. Comparison of the pottery with that from other sites, notably Grave Circle B at Mycenae, indicates that it dates from the Middle Helladic IIIB period (perhaps about 1550 B.C.). Typical and related shapes are the angular bowl or goblet (P 716) and the double-handled kantharos cup (P 708 and 722). The fabric of the spouted beaker (P 723) is related to these. All are of the type traditionally known as yellow Minyan. Another interesting shape, of a fabric with a greenish tint, is the ladle (P 685).

Evidence of burning in the house (some but not all the fragments of vessels like P 708, 716, 724 are burnt) suggests the occurrence of a destruction which shattered the vases, followed by a fire. The absence of signs of violence indicates that natural rather than human agency caused the destruction. It also seems clear that up to the point of that destruction, human activity had been increasing at Nemea even if the settlement had not attained anything like the wealth of nearby Mycenae.

On the bottom shelf, right, of case 12, are artifacts from the successor of the Middle Helladic settlement. These date from the Mycenaean or Late Helladic period (about 1500–1200 B.C.) and include a kylix (P 137), a tripod krater with its bottom pierced for straining (P 75), a ladle (P 85), painted cups (P 78 and 518), and a stirrup jar (P 1407). Once again this is part of the evidence which suggests that Nemea had a small but thriving community during the last phases of the Bronze Age.

On the WALL ABOVE CASE 13 is an aerial photograph taken in 1977 of the Tsoungiza Hill. The houses of the modern village of Archaia Nemea are at the bottom (south); the main prehistoric site of the hill is southwest (below and to the left) of the two chicken coops marked C.

CASE 13: PREHISTORIC AND
GEOMETRIC ARTIFACTS

The left side of case 13 is devoted to material other than pottery groups from the prehistoric period at Nemea. Some of it comes from the area of the Sanctuary of Zeus, but most is from Tsoungiza. It includes many tools such as stone grinders (ST 8, 10, 308, etc.), stone ax heads (ST 289, 2, etc.), and obsidian blades (ST 4, 265, 576–583). From the late Bronze

Fig. 15. Bronze dagger (BR 17).

Age (the Mycenaean period) come the ivory sword pommel (BI 1), the group of terracotta figurines (TC 4, 10, 11, etc.), and the bronze dagger with a bone handle (Fig. 15). Finally there are a few sherds of pottery from the Early Helladic period (roughly the third millennium B.C.) such as P 90, 91, 1370, and so forth. Although this evidence shows clearly that there was human activity at Nemea in the early Bronze Age, it is equally clear that the activity was more limited than that in some earlier and later periods.

The right side of case 13 shows the faint beginnings of activity in the Nemea valley after the hiatus known as the Dark Ages (roughly 1100–700 B.C.). With the fall of Mycenae and the end of Mycenaean civilization in Greece (*ca.* 1150 B.C.) human activity throughout the Balkan peninsula seems to have been much restrained, and the population seems to have dwindled. Not until the 8th century B.C. did Greek civilization begin the renaissance which culminated in the Classical period (480–323 B.C.). Nemea seems to have participated in this reawakening in a limited way. A few examples of fragmentary pottery of the 8th century B.C. have been found close to the Temple and the Altar of Zeus (P 87, 123, 781, 803). These show the characteristic geometric decorative patterns which give the period its name. From this same Geometric period, but discovered in fill washed into the Stadium from the hill above, comes a bronze horse (Fig. 16). A few examples of pottery (P 779 and 380) also date to the 7th century B.C., but clearly Nemea flourished only with the establishment of the games in the 6th century B.C. The traditional date of 573 B.C. coincides well with the evidence of increased activity in the Sanctuary of Zeus.

Fig. 16. Bronze geometric horse (BR 20).

The SOUTHEASTERN CORNER OF THE MAIN EXHIBITION HALL is
devoted to material discovered by the Archaeological Service
of the Ministry of Culture in the valley of ancient Phlious, or
modern Nea Nemea, west of the ancient Nemea valley (see
the map in the courtyard or Fig. 1)—a broad fertile valley that
could support a considerable population. The southern panel
on the island reminds us (with a text in modern Greek) of
other sites known from ancient authors in this valley drained
by the Asopos River, which flows northward to the Gulf of
Corinth. Chief among these sites was Araithyrea, which was
known to Homer (*Iliad* 2.571) and Pausanias (2.12.5). Strabo
(8.6.24) tells us that the inhabitants of Araithyrea abandoned
their town to found Phlious 30 stadia (about 5 km.) away.

Two ancient sites, excavated to varying degrees, might be identified with Araithyrea. One is on the low hill of Aghia Eirene to the left of the road from Nea Nemea to Stymphalia.[33] The foundations of Mycenaean or Late Helladic houses have been discovered here as well as tombs from the end of the Middle Helladic period, one of which is shown during excavation in the photograph to the right of the text on the panel.

The second site is represented by several dozen rock-cut tombs discovered in the modern town of Aidonia, which lies further along on the road to Stymphalia.[34] The tombs themselves have architectural interest, with their long *dromoi,* or entrance passageways (see the photograph on the panel to the right), and their interiors carved out of the soft bedrock to imitate the interiors of houses. These were family tombs in which corpses were buried with pottery, gold jewelry, ivory-inlaid furniture, and so forth. The animals carved on seal stones tell something of the inhabitants' lives, and the scenes on their gold sealing rings tell of their religious liturgies. The scarabs show the existence of trade with and influence from Egypt. Finally, deposits of Geometric pottery show that their descendants continued to venerate the burials made long ago.

CASE 15: JEWELRY FROM AIDONIA

The material in this and the next three cases has not been formally published. Photographs are therefore not allowed, and the following descriptions are necessarily summary and superficial. Case 15 contains material from various tombs at Aidonia: (from left) necklaces, seal stones, gold sealing rings, scarabs, ivory discs once inlaid in wood, gold sew-on rosettes

33. To be published by Z. Aslamantidou.
34. To be published by K. Krystalli-Votsi.

which adorned the clothing of the deceased, bronze and stone arrowheads, stone spindle whorls, and a bronze sword.

CASES 14 AND 16: POTTERY FROM AIDONIA

These two cases display a number of the vases from the Aidonia tombs—only a sample from these rich burials.

CASE 17: POTTERY FROM AGHIA EIRENE

The relatively plain pottery and the terracotta animal figure on the upper right shelf are from the excavations at Aghia Eirene, shown in the photograph mounted on the panel behind the case. Everything else in case 17 comes from the tombs of Aidonia. On the panel to the right is a photograph of one of the Aidonia tombs during excavation.

CASE 18: A NEMEAN WELL AND ARATOS OF SIKYON

This case and the material against the south wall of the room behind it represent the excavation of another well in the Sanctuary of Zeus. Called K 14:4, it is shown in a cross-sectional drawing on the panel to the east (right). It is the nearer of the two wells close to the southwestern corner of the Temple of Zeus, as shown in the photograph on the adjacent panel. (The further well is K 14:3 in case 10; on the site, see p. 128.)

Well K 14:4 was covered with stone slabs at the time of discovery. The uppermost 1.66 m. were empty; the next 3.60 m. were filled with sandy earth containing few artifacts, although two coins found therein are of interest: C 1310, a bronze issue of the Arkadian League of the late 4th century B.C., and C 1287, a bronze issue of Ptolemy III Euergetes of Egypt, dated 247–222 B.C. The sandy earth may have been dumped into the well or, more likely, slowly eroded down into it from between the stone slabs.

The next 2.40 m. of the well were as rich in artifacts·as the upper fill had been poor. This layer of the well represents a period of destruction/cleanup when inscriptions, architectural members, and other debris were dumped deliberately into it. The inscriptions included three large fragments (against the SOUTH WALL) recording a treaty between Argos and Aspendos in the late 4th century B.C. (I 75). This inscription clearly points to control of the sanctuary at the time of the treaty by Argos. The stone was broken elsewhere, for no other fragments were found in the well. The stump of the limestone stele of another inscription, still leaded into its stone base (I 76), also came from this level of the well, as did a major portion of an inscribed marble stele (I 85; the photograph on the wall shows this stele moments after it emerged from the well). The text, in two columns, gives the names of places and people who were the *theorodokoi*, "herald receivers," of the Nemean Games. Every two years when the games were to take place, heralds (*theoroi*) would travel throughout the Greek world to announce the time of the games and the sacred truce surrounding them. Upon arriving at a given town, they would be received by a *theorodokos*, the local representative of the Nemean festival, who would give the *theoroi* shelter, entertainment, and introductions to appropriate officials. This "support group" was probably organized in about 323 B.C. A related text was also found in the well (I 73 + 29; see top shelf, center, case 18). It records that groups of six (*theoroi*?) are to go to various regions of Greece. This inscription, like I 75, must have been broken up elsewhere before being thrown down the well since the smaller of the two joining pieces was discovered in earth fill near the southeastern corner of the Temple of Zeus some 40 m. from the well.

The architectural debris from this well includes a half-finished Ionic-Corinthian column with base (A 146; against the south wall) and, in case 18, painted terracotta simas (AT 69 and 70) and antefixes from the roofs of two different buildings (AT 68 and 78), as well as a fragment of a Corinthian capital (A 147). All this debris suggests that a violent and widespread destruction took place in the sanctuary, a suggestion in no way disproved by the skull of a bull (BI 10), a grinding stone (ST 391), and especially an iron sword with a gold inlaid design near the hilt (IL 296). Mixed in with this debris were bronze rings and attachments from larger vessels (BR 644, 584, 646, 647) and a small bronze locket (BR 648). Pottery such as the lekanis (P 388), bowl (P 381), skyphos (P 382), and askos (P 384) shows that the destruction/cleanup must have taken place in the second half of the 3rd century B.C. This date is confirmed by the silver coin of Sikyon (C 1288), 250–146 B.C., and the bronze coin of Ptolemy III Euergetes (C 1314), 247–222 B.C. A third bronze coin of Corinth (C 1313) cannot be dated so closely, although it clearly belongs in this general period.

At a depth of about 7.66 m. from the mouth of the well, the fill ceased to contain this heavy debris and instead had objects more appropriate to the use of the well as a source of water. This layer, only about 0.20 m. thick, produced two handles (BR 653) from a bronze bucket, or situla, and the bases of two bronze vessels (BR 651 and 652). Another Corinthian bronze coin (C 1312) only generally dates this use of the well, but the pottery, such as a mug (P 386), a kantharos (P 383), and a blisterware jug with impressed ivy-leaf decoration (P 389), belongs to the second half of the 3rd century B.C., though to a period clearly and necessarily earlier than that of the material in the layer just above.

The final 0.15 m. of the well also produced several elements of bronze vessels: a rim (BR 649), a handle (BR 654), and four bases (BR 650, 652, 656, 657), again indicating a period of

use. The date of this use which emerges from a fish plate
(P 391) and a cup-kantharos with stamped decoration on its
floor (P 385) is the late 4th century B.C.

All these data together give us the history of both the well
and the Sanctuary of Zeus at Nemea. The well was constructed in the late 4th century B.C., at the same time as many
other buildings (the Temple of Zeus, the Stadium, the Xenon,
the Bath, etc.). Clearly this is the time when the games returned to Nemea, probably under Macedonian influence (see
case 3, pp. 22–23). Then a gap in the use of the well reflects
the shift of the games from Nemea to Argos, which appears
from other evidence in the sanctuary to have occurred in the
270s B.C. Next comes a period of use in the second half of the
3rd century which must reflect renewed activity at the site,
followed by a cleanup after a violent destruction. Written
sources tell of an episode in the history of the Nemean Games
which can explain these data. Aratos of Sikyon, at odds with
Argos, reestablished the Nemean Games at Nemea in about
235 B.C. and blockaded those which took place the same year
at Argos.[35] Any athlete who insisted on participating in the
games at Argos was captured and sold into slavery, in ob-
vious violation of the sacred truce. We do not know how
many years Aratos's games took place at Nemea, for when
Aratos later became allied with Argos, the "alternate" games
were disbanded; but the second use of the well can safely be
associated with the reestablishment of the games at Nemea.
The violent destruction would have resulted from this episode, and the Argive inscriptions may have been deliberately
broken up by the Sikyonians and the buildings destroyed either by them or by the returning Argives, who dumped the
material down the well, thus effectively cutting off the water
supply of the sanctuary and making imitations of Aratos's alternate games in the future difficult at best. As we shall see

35. Plutarch, *Aratos* 28.3–4.

shortly, this was not the only time when violence entered the
sacred "apolitical" Panhellenic festival center.

CASE 19: THE EARLY TEMPLE OF ZEUS AND
VIOLENCE AT THE NEMEAN GAMES

This section of the exhibition deals with the Early Temple of
Zeus and its destruction. As will be seen at the site itself, the
Early Temple lies completely under the 4th-century Temple
of Zeus and has been almost completely obliterated by it.
Nonetheless, the architecture of the building has not been
completely lost. The 4th-century Temple cuts through layers
of limestone working chips which lie north and south of it;
these layers date from the 6th century B.C. and thus predate
and are irrelevant to the 4th-century Temple. The sixth-
century date is appropriate for the temple of a festival organized in 573 B.C. The bottom shelf, left, of case 19 holds
several fragments of roof tiles from that initial period of the
Early Temple. These include fragments of hip tiles (AT 95 and
232) and pan tiles with the stamps of manufacturers on them:
rosette (AT 245), "key hole" (AT 205), and "S" (AT 224). On
the shelf above these pieces are a Corinthian cover tile with
notches cut out at one end (AT 106) and antefixes (Fig. 17)
with impressed decoration on the front (AT 82 and 91; rosettes
are stamped on their upper surfaces).[36] These elements have
been put together to reconstruct the roof of the Early Temple
as it appeared at the western end. The life-sized MODEL OF THE
ROOF near the door to the courtyard (note the drawing on the
wall above) shows a regular Corinthian tile system with large
square pan tiles the joints of which are protected by peaked,
rectilinear cover tiles. The Early Temple, like many temples

36. For similar antefixes of similar date see C. K. Williams, "Demaratus and
Early Corinthian Roofs," ΣΤΗΛΗ (Τόμος εἰς μνήμην N. Κοντολέοντος,
Athens 1978) 345–50.

Fig. 17. An impressed terracotta antefix from the
Early Temple of Zeus (AT 91).

of this period elsewhere (notably at Isthmia and at Corinth)[37]
but unlike temples of later date, did not have gables or pediments at both ends; rather, its western (back) end was enclosed by a hipped roof. The handling of the oblique joint between the side and end roofs differed from site to site, but
here at Nemea the solution was simple: during manufacture,
while the clay was damp, a Corinthian pan tile was bent on
the diagonal to accommodate the adjacent pan tiles on each
side. The drawing and the model show how this system
worked. Extant tile fragments are indicated in red-orange on
the model and their inventory numbers noted. Many of them
are on display in case 19.

In the middle of the top shelf is another curiosity of the
Early Temple: a fragment of cement with a stucco coating on
one side (AT 173). Many such fragments have been found
with the debris of the Early Temple, and it is not known
whether they came from the floor or the walls or some other
part of the building. Clearly, however, the Greeks of the

37. O. Broneer, *Isthmia* I, *Temple of Poseidon* (Princeton 1971) 40–53.

6th century B.C. knew how to make and use cement because a similar cement adheres to the undersurface of the original tiles, for which it seems to have served as a bedding. (Such cement should be distinguished from the structural concrete of the Roman age.)

The top and bottom shelves, right, of case 19 hold fragments from the ridge akroteria which once sat on the roof of the Early Temple (Fig. 18). As can be seen from the pieces on the bottom shelf (AT 117 and 119), the base of these akroteria consisted of a Corinthian cover tile bent down at either end to follow the adjacent sloping sides of the roof. The finial resting on this base was painted vividly on both sides with a double volute above which was a palmette with alternating deep red and black leaves (compare with the drawing on the wall to the right). The heart of the palmette was cut out so that when it was in position on the peak of the roof, blue sky was visible at its core. Although these akroteria were discovered with the other roofing materials of the Early Temple, their style indicates that they were part of a late Archaic (perhaps ca. 500 B.C.) repair or refurbishing of the Early Temple.

In addition to these elements, dozens of limestone blocks from the Early Temple have been found at Nemea, both in the destruction debris of that building and, reused, in later construction (e.g., as wellheads L 17:2 and K 14:3, in cases 9 and 10). These blocks are characteristically 0.31–0.32 m. high, 0.88 m. wide, and 0.92–0.93 m. long. Near one end of the top surface is almost always a set of "ice-tong" holes used to lift the stone into position during the construction of the Early Temple. On the BASE TO THE RIGHT OF CASE 19 are two blocks from this series (A 163 and 171). One of them (A 163) preserves the lifting holes, and both have been cut down to receive wooden beams. Presumably these blocks came from near the top of the wall.

Like many other elements of the Early Temple, these two blocks have been badly burnt and broken, and one can see

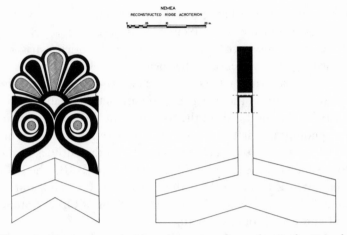

Fig. 18. Reconstructed ridge akroterion from the Early Temple of Zeus.

how the stone has been blackened by fire. Two photographs on the wall above them show part of the destruction debris of the Early Temple. On the top shelf, center, of case 19 are two examples of the twisted and vitrified tiles of the Early Temple which have also been found in this debris (AT 93 and 115). They show clearly the violent end of the Early Temple. In addition, these layers of debris have produced many bronze arrowheads, some of which are displayed here (BR 77, 113, 162, etc.), and iron spear points and butts (IL 116, 174, etc.). These show with equal clarity that the cause of the destruction was a pitched battle whose date, on the basis of pottery in the debris, can be assigned to the final quarter of the 5th century B.C., probably in the period 415–410 B.C.[38] Another

38. Although no ancient author records such a battle, Thucydides does attest to extensive military maneuvering in Nemea and its environs in 419/8 B.C. (5.58–60) and again in 415/4 B.C. (6.95). These seem the likely years when control of the Nemean Games, and of the Sanctuary of Zeus, passed from Kleonai to Argos. On this question see S. G. Miller, "Kleonai, the Nemean Games, and the Lamian War," *Hesperia*, suppl. 20 (1982) 100–108.

consequence of this battle was almost certainly the removal of the Nemean Games from Nemea until the 330s B.C. (cf. case 9, p. 43). Thus once again archaeological evidence has revealed political violence in the ancient Panhellenic centers.

On the SOUTH WALL to the right (west) of the door to the courtyard and on the panels beyond are details of ancient activity on the south side of the Sanctuary of Zeus, as shown in the photograph at the top of the northernmost panel. This aerial view (Fig. 19), taken in 1984, shows the outlines of the foundations of the *oikoi* (A–A), of the Xenon (B–B), the Bath (then with a shed over the bathing chamber, C), and a unit of kilns (D). It also records the pits in the floor of Oikoi 8 and 9 and in the area south of them.

On the bottom of this panel is a photograph of one room in the Xenon with a stone-paved hearth (see Fig. 32). More will be said about this building during the discussion of the site.

The central panel displays photographs of the bathing chamber of the Bath during its original excavation in 1924. On the right is a view of the eastern tubs. On the upper left is a detail of those tubs, and on the lower left a more general view, with the steps down into the chamber on the left, a column drum, and—to the right at middle ground—some of the parapet slabs which will be seen in the Bath itself.

Photographs on the panel to the left, near the south wall, show the water reservoirs south of the Bath at the time of their discovery in 1982. These too will be visible at the site.

Sometime during the third quarter of the 5th century B.C., Oikoi 8 and 9 and the area south of them were taken over by a bronze sculptor. The pits visible in the aerial view of the south side of the sanctuary are the remains of his workshop. On the south wall near the last panel are two color photographs of this site. Here, at the top, was the furnace where he melted bronze before pouring it into his molds (see Fig. 59). The lower photograph shows one of these molds (TC 59) still in place in the pit. The large stone basin here, also from the

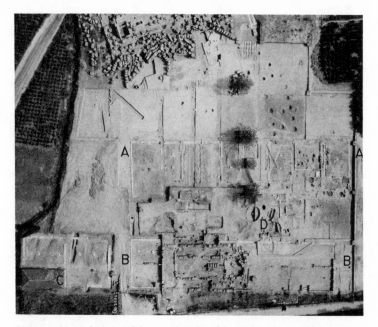

Fig. 19. Aerial view of the south side of the Sanctuary of Zeus, 1980.

workshop (ST 362), was apparently used to mix clay for the molds.

CASE 20: INDUSTRY AND TECHNOLOGY

On the left are artifacts from the sculptor's workshop. Three terracotta molds are displayed: TC 60, for the shoulder of a statue at the neck; TC 59 for an arm; and TC 57 for the drapery on a relatively flat part of the upper body. The statue was made in pieces (legs, arms, feet, head, etc.) by the lost-wax process; fragments of such pieces are in cases 6 and 7. A core was made of clay with a skeleton of iron armatures such as IL 39, 42 a–b, and 49 here. Wax was applied to this core and shaped as desired. Details were worked out with tools like the pointed stone inscriber (ST 342). Damp clay, perhaps after an initial working in a lekanis like TC 192, was applied over the wax, forming a negative impression of it. The whole was then set into its own pit, where a fire around the mold baked the clay and melted the wax, which flowed out of a hole left for the purpose. The molten bronze poured into the space left by the wax cooled and hardened in the shape originally formed by the wax. The molds were broken and the bronze pieces removed to be soldered together with lead from ingots such as IL 31. The bronze was then worked over with tools such as the chisels, drills, and hammer found in the workshop (IL 11, 12, 14, 15, 60, 476) and smoothed and polished with stone grinders such as ST 341. After the finished statue was leaded into a base (like those previously seen on the north wall near case 7), it was dedicated to Zeus.

Photographs on the SOUTH WALL of the room show the complex of kilns along the north wall of the Xenon and east of the Basilica (see the aerial photograph on the first panel above). The first photograph is a general view of the kilns from the west. The north wall of the Xenon is marked B at the right; the nearest of the kilns is a circular example marked K. In the distance is the settling tank for clay, marked S. Between K and S are two more kilns, both rectilinear, with the southern one (L) the better preserved. The next photograph shows the rectilinear kilns from the north with the settling tank (S) at the left. Note the steps which lead down into it. Kiln L, with the firing-chamber floor preserved, is in the middle ground; the north wall of the Xenon cuts through it. The third photograph in the series, in color, shows the entrances to the stoking chamber of kiln L. Both this kiln and the less well preserved one to the north had stoking chambers entered by a common sunken area where fuel was stored. The next two photographs show kiln L from the south and from above (west). Finally, a drawing by C. K. Williams (Fig. 20) shows kiln L as discovered (upper left) and with the firing chamber partially restored (upper right).

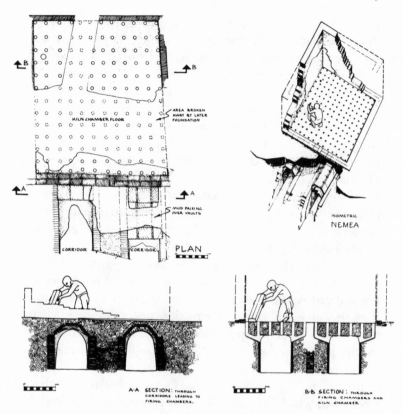

Fig. 20. Kiln, by C. K. Williams.

All these kilns belong to the last thirty years of the 4th century B.C. and were used exclusively, so far as the materials found in them allow us to say, for the manufacture of roof tiles. In case 20 (center) are examples of the tripod stacking dividers (TC 14 and 22) which allowed the hot air of the firing chamber to circulate between the stacked tiles, baking them evenly. The fragment of another such divider made in the form of a finger (TC 13) reveals a certain humor, perhaps born of the tedium of making hundreds of such dividers. Beside this are examples of wedge separators (TC 15, 21, 23) used to keep the stacks of tiles separate from one another. These kilns

were used to make the tiles of the 4th-century Temple of
Zeus, the Bath, the Xenon, the houses south of the Xenon,
and (we may assume) other buildings still to be discovered.
They seem to have been laid out slightly in error, since the
Xenon cuts through the one kiln (L), and the circular kiln
west of it was apparently built after the construction of the
Xenon was under way—to finish the job. This extensive
complex shows, first, that there was a massive construction
program in the final decades of the 4th century at Nemea—
the time when the games returned to Nemea and such a program would have been necessary. The massiveness of the program speaks vividly to the funding poured into the effort; the
suggestion (see p. 23) that the Macedonians were responsible
seems inevitable. Who else at that time could have mustered
such funding? The construction complex shows, second, that
roof tiles were made on the spot for construction projects,
not ordered ready-made from a central supplier. This situation, though it differs from the modern one, is logical in view
of the problems of transport and breakage. It would have been
much easier to import clay to Nemea than to have brought in
ready-made tiles.

In case 20, right (east), is a series of tools from another
workshop, which, like the kilns, was between the Xenon and
the *oikoi,* but further west, just north of (and partly covered
over by) the narthex of the Basilica. Here were informal pits
filled with chips from the working of Pentelic marble which
was used, so far as is known today, only on the sima of the
4th-century Temple of Zeus. It may well have been here that
the sima was carved (see the courtyard, northeastern corner).
Bronze tweezers (BR 49 and 908) found here would have been
useful in such an operation, nor is the ivory stylus (BI 13) out
of place. That the work which took place here was specifically sacred is attested by the lead sheet (IL 279) once nailed to
the end of a wooden beam or something similar. It bears the
inscription IEPO(Y), "of the sanctuary." The black-glaze

plate with stamped decoration and rouletting on its floor
(P 370), the bowl with similar decoration (P 369), and the two
lamps (L 39 and 40) which were found with the marble chips
date from the period between 350 and 325 B.C., an appropriate date for the major construction program the centerpiece
of which was the Temple of Zeus.

The remaining objects in the right side of case 20 are from
the 4th-century Temple of Zeus itself. IL 236 is an iron dowel
with some of the lead which held it in place still adhering to
it. Blocks in the wall and the superstructure of the Temple
were fastened to the block immediately below by means of
these dowels. The tools (chisel, point, etc.) were discovered
in the layers of limestone chips from the construction of the
Temple (IL 308, 377, 505), as were the lead ingots, IL 335 and
242, the second with the enigmatic inscription ΛΑΚΤ.

On the wall to the right between case 20 and the DOOR TO
THE COURTYARD is a large terracotta akroterion (AT 42). It features a crowning palmette above intricate volutes in the center
of which is a siren. Dating from the first half, and probably
the second quarter, of the 5th century B.C., this akroterion
was the central roof decoration of Oikos 9 (a small model of
this *oikos* is beneath the siren).

The Courtyard

In the courtyard itself, at the northwestern corner to the right
of the foyer window, are two Ionic engaged half columns
with molded bases (A 128 and 129). These are the first of several pieces which allow us to reconstruct Oikos 9, at least on
paper (see Fig. 60). Oikos 9, like the other eight *oikoi,* was
first constructed in the period just after the Greek victory in
the Persian Wars (i.e., 480–460 B.C.). Again like the other
oikoi, it was severely damaged when the Sanctuary of Zeus
was destroyed late in the 5th century B.C. (see p. 61). Unlike

the other *oikoi*, it was not reconstructed in the late 4th century; its abandonment and burial at that time account for the relative wealth of architectural elements which have survived from it (and for the absence of Oikos 9 on the model of the Sanctuary of Zeus at 300 B.C.).

The surface of the projecting rectilinear wings of columns A 128 and 129 is characterized by *anathyrosis*, the surface treatment of stone whereby a band at the edge is worked smooth to allow a close join with an adjacent block and the surface of the stone further from the edge is roughly picked to a depth that prevents contact with the next block. The presence of *anathyrosis* means that the blocks were part of a wall, so that the lowest level of the facade of Oikos 9 was a solid wall from which columns projected at intervals.

In the northwestern corner of the courtyard is a Doric capital from an *anta*, the end of a wall enlarged to correspond to one or more columns continuing the line of the wall. Because this building had an *anta*, it could not have been surrounded by columns but rather would have had columns only across the facade, though other reconstructions are theoretically possible. The badly burnt upper surface of the capital indicates that the superstructure of the building was wood and that the building was destroyed by fire.

To the right (east) of the corner of the courtyard is an Ionic half capital (A 132) which clearly belongs to the series of columns noted in the preceding paragraph. The tops of the flutes are curiously treated, having little tongues of stone, a stylistic detail usually found in the western Greek world (e.g., at Corfu). The eyes of the volutes are rough picked for the adhesion of coarse plaster; marble-dust plaster originally covered the whole. Again the upper surface is burnt.

The drawing of a reconstruction of Oikos 9 (see Fig. 60) on the courtyard wall to the right clarifies the following reconstruction details. The *anta* capital (A 133) would have been

on a side wall just behind a corner column and therefore not
visible in this view of the facade.

Below the reconstruction are four more Ionic half columns
from Oikos 9, each of which adds to the picture. The first (A
131), on the basis of its diminished width, is from higher on
the facade than the bases A 128 and 129. It exhibits a square
empolion cutting for the attachment of another piece above.
Unlike the columns with *anathyrosis* on their sides, this one
has plaster and was therefore not part of a solid wall. Further,
it has cuttings on the side for a metal grille. Thus windows
with bronze grilles have been restored in the upper register of
the facade of Oikos 9.

The next column fragment (A 241) is broken across the
top, but *anathyrosis* on it shows that it came from relatively
low in the column.

The next column (A 240), like the first to the left, has an
empolion cutting and a setting line on its top surface for use as
a guide during construction. More important, however, is
the *anathyrosis* on the left below a cutback to a smooth surface, which has a cutting for a metal grille. In other words,
this piece comes from the window line; its width vis-à-vis
that of the lower columns and the capitals allows its height to
be established within narrow limits. In addition, because the
right side of this piece is covered with plaster, the column itself was at an opening. We therefore place it just to the left (as
we face it) of the central intercolumniation of the facade.

The next column fragment (A 130) is battered, but it exhibits an *empolion* cutting which is oblique rather than parallel
to the line of the wall like the previous examples. If there
were extant another element with a lower *empolion* cutting
like this, the two pieces would clearly be reconstructed the
one on top of the other.

Finally we come to the Ionic corner capital (Fig. 21), which
tells us that the whole facade of Oikos 9 had six columns

Fig. 21. Corner Ionic capital from Oikos 9 (A 244).

rather than four columns within *antae*. Its volute eyes are cut out in sockets for the attachment of the final decoration rather than roughly picked like the surface on A 132. Moreover, its upper surface is heavily burnt. There can now be little question that the superstructure of Oikos 9 was wood.

These fragments convey an image of Oikos 9 as a building with an elaborate but not heavily constructed facade. From the remains in the field, we know that its back walls were mud brick on a stone socle. A light and airy shelter during the time of the games, it could have been locked for protection at other times. If the other *oikoi* were the same, we could envision them as a row of buildings with fancy fronts and plain back rooms—like a Hollywood Main Street set for an Old West town.

Each *oikos* was almost certainly the dedication of an individual city-state. A block of limestone in the courtyard NEAR THE DOOR to the main exhibition hall bears the inscription ΡΟΔΙΩΝ, "of the Rhodians" (I 105; see also p. 119). It is not difficult to imagine this stone standing outside one of the *oikoi,* proclaiming its dedicators to the world. This inscription, however, dates from the late 4th century B.C. and cannot belong to Oikos 9. But a 5th-century B.C. block reused in a wall of the Xenon bears the inscription ΕΠΙΔΑΥΡΙΩΝ, "of the Epidaurians" (I 31; see p. 169). This might have been the block which stood outside Oikos 9.

A photograph on the wall of the courtyard above I 105, taken from atop the columns of the Temple of Zeus, looking southeast (see Fig. 57), shows the open square bounded by the *oikoi,* including Oikos 9, which is so labeled.

On the OTHER SIDE OF THE DOOR to the main exhibition hall are architectural elements from the Temple of Zeus. Although the Temple is best studied on the site, some parts of it have to be displayed here. On the wall is a photograph, taken from the south, of the crypt at the western end of the Temple. Both the stairs into the crypt and the wall of the Early Temple running beneath the stairs alongside the north wall can be seen.

Below the photograph is a Corinthian capital (A 16) from the lower interior order of the Temple, like the example in the foyer (A 20); north of the east door to the courtyard is another capital (A 18). To the right (east) are two Corinthian column shafts with their molded bases (A 248 and 99), above which on the wall are long and short cross sections of the restored Temple showing the position of the lower Corinthian and the upper Ionic columns. Next on the wall is a drawing of an Ionic capital from the interior upper order of the Temple. Below this are two engaged Ionic half columns from the upper order (A 11 and 249) flanking an engaged Ionic quarter column from the corner of the interior upper order.

Along the EAST WALL OF THE COURTYARD pieces of the marble sima, or gutter, are displayed, along with marble antefixes from the Temple of Zeus (A 3, 5 a–e, 6), the only marble (Pentelic) elements in the building. The antefixes are carved with a simple palmette, and the center of each sima block is decorated with nicely wrought lion's head spouts (see Fig. 53). From the lions' heads spring acanthus tendrils, which spiral to an end beneath the antefix. On the base below the sima are drawings of a section through a lion's head, a typical restored sima block, and the restored south colonnade of the Temple of Zeus, showing the location of the sima vis-à-vis the remainder of the building (see Fig. 52).

Above the marble sima, the roof of the Temple was covered with typical Corinthian terracotta tiles; an example, a pan tile (AT 19), is displayed at the east door to the courtyard.

Along the east side of the courtyard SOUTH OF THE DOOR is an unfinished limestone Corinthian or Ionic column shaft (A 138) on which the base molding has been worked but not the vertical flutes. Chisel marks on the moldings as well as markings on the bottom of the base show that this column was wrought by turning it on a lathe. A photograph on the wall above the column shows how it was discovered in use as a cover for a well.

The rectilinear block beyond the column bears the inscription ΕΦΟΔΙΑΙ (I 8). It may come from an enclosure sacred to Artemis Ephodia or Hekate Ephodia and dates from the early 5th century B.C.[39]

Next is a small circular altar with a depression on the top and an inscription ΔΙϜΟΣ ΕΝΣΙΤΑΡΧΙΟΥ (I 9) of the late 4th century B.C. The second word, otherwise unknown, seems to indicate that the altar belonged to Zeus in the Grain Office.[40]

In the SOUTHEASTERN CORNER OF THE COURTYARD is a circular triglyph-metope altar with its base (A 71 and 70 a–b) from the early Hellenistic period. It was discovered plowed

39. IG IV.484.

40. This altar was briefly published by N. Verdelis, M. Jameson, and I. Papachristodoulou, "Ἀρχαϊκαὶ ἐπιγραφαὶ ἐκ Τίρυνθος," Ἀρχ. Ἐφ. (1975) 198–99; cf. SEG 30.531, where the altar is wrongly stated to have been found in the Xenon. It was probably discovered in 1958 south of the Bath.

up by modern agricultural activity about 35 m. northeast of the Temple of Zeus.

Along the south wall are two architectural fragments of early Hellenistic date: a Doric epistyle block (A 179) which was found near, and may be from, the Xenon and a Doric triglyph-metope frieze block (A 188) found south of the Bath but in a late context.

The Doric Capital (A 7) shown in a 1924 photograph on the wall above was found in the Bath and probably belonged to one of its interior columns. The Doric column drum (A 82) that now supports the capital was found in a well north of the Xenon. It is too big for the capital and not to be associated with it.

Next, the octagonal Doric capital (A 30) resting on an octagonal column shaft from the interior of the Xenon (A 181) dates, like the Xenon, to the late 4th century B.C.

At the south door of the courtyard is a votive Doric capital which once carried a statue (A 27). On top it has both a dowel hole and a circular setting line for the statue plinth; stylistically, the rounding of the abacus, the top element in a Doric capital, is curious (contrast with capital A 7 to the left). The echinus, the element below the abacus, also has curious horizontal facets on its face, one of them inscribed in retrograde letters of the 6th century B.C.: MANION—. Presumably this was part of the name of the man who dedicated the statue with its capital base.

The SOUTHWESTERN PART OF THE COURTYARD is devoted to material from sites outside the Nemea valley. A map near the corner indicates the location of places already mentioned—Argos, Kleonai, Phlious, Aghia Eirene, and Λιdonia—as well as those still to be discussed (see Fig. 1).

Between the south door of the courtyard and the corner are four blocks from the wall of an Archaic building at Phlious. The cut grooves for lifting these blocks with ropes are characteristic of this period. Although the building from which these blocks come is unknown, it was probably sacred, for its walls were covered with Archaic, early Roman, and Byzantine inscriptions.[41]

The marble capital of the 2nd or 3rd century after Christ in the southwestern corner of the courtyard was found in the modern village of Petri on the northwestern edge of the Phlious plain.

In front of the foyer windows on the west wall of the courtyard are two limestone slabs with elegiac verses inscribed in the 2nd century after Christ.[42] According to the inscriptions, portraits of a certain Flavian (on the right) and his wife, Silvia (on the left), were inserted in the cuttings on the tops of these blocks. These are probably the very portraits, also found at Petri, which are now in the museum at Nauplion.

NORTH OF THE DOOR from the courtyard to the foyer is a marble base with the legs of a dog. Two fragments from a small marble statue are displayed with it: the base and legs and also the torso of a youth striding vigorously forward.[43] Of the Roman period, all these pieces were found south of the Nemea valley in a Roman villa overlooking the Tretos pass (near the modern hamlet Hani Anesti), which leads to the Argive plain.

41. R. L. Scranton, "Inscriptions from Phlius," *Hesperia* 5 (1936) 234–46 (= *SEG* 11.275).

42. To be published by Ch. Kritzas.

43. To be published by An. Delivorrias.

IV

THE SANCTUARY
OF ZEUS

The Houses

A flagstone path links the museum and the Temple of Zeus
north of it. After descending a few steps into the excavation
zone, the path continues northward between ancient buildings to an abrupt westward turn (Fig. 22). These buildings are
large complex structures built up against one another except
where the narrow path runs between them. Facing north onto
an ancient east-west road, the gravel layers of which are below the modern path, these units were built mostly in the last
quarter of the 4th century B.C. and were out of use by the

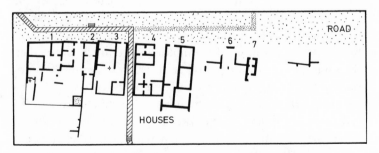

Fig. 22. Detail of the general site plan, showing houses.

middle of the 3rd century or earlier. In the second half of the 3rd century a small isolated area to the east was built over and used briefly; in the 2nd century B.C. an equally small and isolated region to the west in House 1 was reused. The shift of the Nemean Games to Argos is made dramatically clear in this region (see p. 57).

These structures have been labeled houses because of the domestic character of their contents. For example, evidence of cooking was discovered in one room of House 4 (the second room east of the turn in the path): a small stand for the support of cooking pottery, made of three Lakonian tiles placed on edge to form a vertical vent. Some of the ash and burnt earth surrounding these tiles remained as a kind of plaster on the adjacent walls (Fig. 23). Similarly, in several other rooms of these houses, hearths or other evidence of cooking was discovered. The well in House 3 (to the southwest) also suggests a domestic function. It is marked by a large square block into which the circular mouth has been carved. (The shaft of the well is lined with rubble construction to a depth of 5.75 m., after which it continues unlined to a depth of 7.10 m.)

If hearths and a well suggest domestic uses, still the walls of the houses, especially along the facade, were built of blocks larger than those commonly used for houses. In other places (the north-south wall of House 4 immediately east of the path) the top of the rubble wall is covered with tiles which served as a leveling course for mud-brick or adobe walls higher up. In addition, these buildings are much larger than the typical house of the period at other sites, and they do not present the stratigraphic accumulation one expects in the domestic quarters of a true habitation. That they were an official, albeit subsidiary, part of the Sanctuary of Zeus is evident in the artifacts discovered in them which are labeled as belonging to Zeus, such as the mug in case 6 of the museum (P 778; see p. 32), or in other artifacts which are official by

Fig. 23. Cooking stand in House 4, with marble relief (ss 8, now in the museum) still *in situ* in the foreground, from the south.

their nature, such as a bronze weight of Argos (Fig. 24).[44] These houses, then, are perhaps best interpreted as the official quarters of priests or judges (the *Hellanodikai*) or caretakers of the sanctuary during the biennial games, not as the domiciles of a permanent population at Nemea during the Classical or Hellenistic periods.

Fig. 24. Bronze weight (BR 1194).

44. Such items show clearly that Argos was in control of the Nemean Games in the Hellenistic period; see pp. 20, 57, 61–62.

The Basilica and the
Early Christian Community

To find a settlement of permanent residents who lived, worked, and died on the site, we must look back to the Neolithic and Bronze ages or ahead to the later history of the Nemea valley and the small farming community of Early Christians which grew up among the ruins of the ancient sanctuary in the 5th and 6th centuries after Christ.[45]

When the flagstone path turns left, it follows the line of the main ancient east-west road through the valley. In the distance to the north are the three standing columns of the Temple of Zeus; but just north of the path, about chest high, are the remains of the Basilica which served as a focus for the Early Christian community. Beneath these remains are those of the Xenon. A short distance further on the path, cut into a wall and protected by a modern cover, is a Christian burial typical of those found at Nemea. In a grave lined and covered with rough stone slabs, the body was laid with the head at the west, propped up to face east in characteristic fashion, awaiting the Resurrection and the Last Judgment. (See p. 93 for a general discussion of Early Christian burials.)

Beyond the grave, a short flight of modern steps leads up to the level of the floor of the Basilica, from which the remains are best viewed.

The Basilica was first excavated in 1924. Shortly thereafter, a large quantity of stone, once part of the fabric of the build-

---

45. The geographer Strabo places between Phlious and Kleonai both the Sacred Grove of Nemea and a village (kome) called Bembina. The village was apparently quite old since it was already known to the fifth-century B.C. historian and ethnographer Hellanikos (who calls it a city [polis] rather than a village and gives the name as Bembinon) and his contemporary the epic poet Panyassis, uncle of Herodotus (who speaks of Herakles' battle with the "Bembinatin lion"), both of whom are cited by Stephanus of Byzantium, a scholar and antiquarian of the 5th century after Christ (Ethnika, s.v. Bembina). No trace of this Bembina or Bembinon has ever been found, however, and despite the testimony of Strabo

ing, was removed and used in the construction of a protective shed which stood until 1987 over the southwestern part of the Bath. This plundering of a Christian building in the interests of preserving pagan antiquities was carried out with a certain ironic propriety, since the Early Christians themselves had plundered the Temple of Zeus and other pagan monuments in the sanctuary in order to construct their Basilica. Together with the removal of additional blocks to the museum and the more haphazard destruction resulting from sixty years of exposure, however, this plundering has undoubtedly left the remains of the Basilica less easy to understand and appreciate today. Furthermore, most of the interior of the Basilica has been excavated far below the original floor level in order to reveal parts of the ancient Xenon which lies directly beneath it. As a result, the site occupied by these two buildings can seem at first a confusing jumble of walls running in all directions. With the help of the aerial photograph (Fig. 25) and the plans (Fig. 26; see also Fig. 30), however, and by observing that the reused wall blocks of Temple limestone resting on the Basilica foundations have weathered to a dark gray and lie at a higher level than the lower, mostly lighter colored, poros and rubble walls of the Xenon, we can follow the lines of the Christian building with some confidence.

The original basic plan (Fig. 26) is simple. A broad central nave (*ca.* 23.50 m. long and 7.50 m. wide) is flanked by aisles the same length, each roughly half the width of the nave (*ca.* 3.50 m.). The nave ends in an apse, which projects beyond the straight eastern walls of the aisles and increases the

---

the town may have been located some distance from the Sanctuary of Zeus, perhaps even outside the Nemea valley. Cf. the statement of Pliny the Elder (*NH* 4.6.21) that the *regio Nemea* between Kleonai and Kleitor—a distance of some forty miles—was known as Bembinadia; it is by no means clear where in all this area, which contains several important ancient sites, the town of Bembina itself was to be found. For the moment we can say only that no evidence of a regularly inhabited site of Classical, Hellenistic, or early Roman date has been found in the valley.

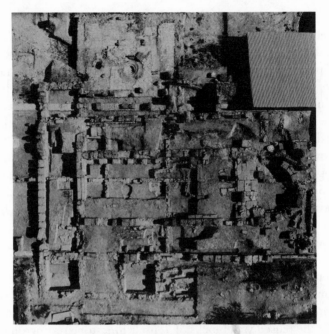

Fig. 25. Aerial view of the Basilica, 1980.

length of the Basilica by 4.50 m. West of and perpendicular to
the nave and aisles lies the narthex (*ca.* 16.50 by 4.50 m.), the
lines of which are extended north and south beyond the aisle
walls by two small side rooms (each *ca.* 4.50 m. square).
Typical of small local churches of the 5th and 6th centuries
throughout Greece, the plan as well as the size is also similar
to the remains of a basilica (Fig. 27) at the top of Evangelistria
Hill, the prominent peak south of the sanctuary easily identified by the modern chapel at its summit. This chapel in fact
lies adjacent to the Early Christian church, which has been
partly investigated but remains virtually unpublished.[46]

46. A short paragraph of description and a small plan (Fig. 27 here) were
published by A. C. Orlandos in *Actes du Ve congrès international d'archéologie
chrétienne, 1954* (Paris 1957) 112.

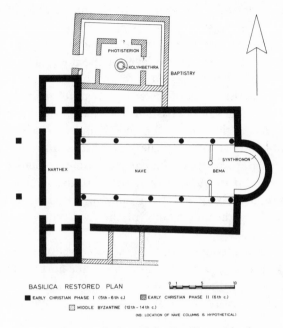

PHOTISTERION

KOLYMBETHRA

BAPTISTRY

SYNTHRONON

NARTHEX   NAVE   BEMA

BASILICA   RESTORED   PLAN

■ EARLY CHRISTIAN PHASE I (5th - 6th c.)   ▨ EARLY CHRISTIAN PHASE II (6th c.)

▦ MIDDLE   BYZANTINE   (12th - 14th c.)

(NB: LOCATION OF NAVE COLUMNS IS HYPOTHETICAL)

Fig. 26. Restored plan of the Basilica with phases.

We begin a more detailed examination of the valley Basilica at its western end,[47] where the west wall of the narthex provides a good illustration of the types of construction used in the building. The foundations are of rubble, a mixture of unworked fieldstones, fragments of earlier buildings, and terracotta tiles, all set in a matrix of strong cement. Above them rose the Basilica walls proper, constructed of cut limestone

47. For detailed discussion of the Early Christian basilicas in Greece and fuller treatment of individual features mentioned briefly in the following description, see A. C. Orlandos, Ἡ ξυλόστεγος παλαιοχριστιανικὴ βασιλικὴ τῆς μεσογειακῆς λεκάνης (Βιβλ. ᾿Αθ. ᾿Αρχ. ᾿Ετ. 35: Athens 1952); and G. A. Soteriou, Αἱ χριστιανικαὶ Θῆβαι τῆς Θεσσαλίας καὶ αἱ παλαιοχριστιανικαὶ βασιλικαὶ τῆς Ἑλλάδος (Athens 1929 = ᾿Αρχ. ᾿Εφ. 1929), and Χριστιανικὴ καὶ Βυζαντινὴ ᾿Αρχαιολογία[2] I (Athens 1962). Also useful for more recent discoveries is D. Pallas, Les monuments paleochrétiens de Grèce découverts de 1959 à 1973 (Rome 1977).

blocks laboriously transported from the Temple of Zeus;
along the western side of the narthex, as at most points in the
Basilica, little more than a single course of this wall is preserved, more or less at the level of the floor. The masons'
marks—small letters carved into the upper surface of the
blocks along the center of the wall—are unrelated to the position of the blocks in the Basilica; they date instead from their
original use in the cella wall of the Temple. Considering the
difficulty and expense of hauling good stone into the Nemea
valley and the poverty of the Early Christian settlement here,
it is hardly surprising that the remains of the ancient sanctuary were actively quarried for building material, a practice
continued by the inhabitants of the local villages into the
present century.

The narthex contains the largest preserved patches of terracotta tile paving in the Basilica, one in the northeastern corner, another further south, midway between the east and west
walls; a few fragments are also visible elsewhere in the building. This paving, composed of yellowish orange tiles roughly
0.30 m. square (an example is displayed in the museum; see
case 11, p. 47), once covered the whole of the narthex, nave,
and aisles. It was badly damaged in places by medieval graves
which cut through it, and some of it had to be removed when
excavation inside the Basilica continued below the floor level.

The narthex, an invariable feature of Early Christian basilicas in Greece, served as a vestibule for the church. It communicated with the nave and aisles through three doors in its east
wall; the thresholds of two (those leading to the nave and the
north aisle) are preserved. The central doorway was naturally
the most important: considerably wider (nearly 3.00 m.) than
the others, it had a threshold constructed of three reworked
ancient blocks, the westernmost of which is now cracked.
Two doorways in the west wall of the narthex, one opposite
the entrance to each of the aisles, provided access from the
outside. The threshold block of the south door now sits

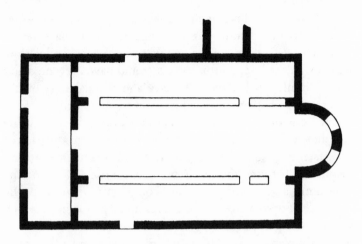

Fig. 27. Sketch plan of basilica on the Evangelistria Hill, from A. C. Orlandos, *Actes du Ve congrès international d'archéologie chrétienne, 1954* (Paris 1957) 112.

slightly askew on the foundations of the outer wall; that of the north door is missing.

Threshold blocks are also visible in the north and south walls of the narthex at the entrance to each of the small square rooms. The precise function of these rooms is unknown, and they may have been used for a variety of purposes. The southern one in particular, perhaps in conjunction with the slightly later room adjoining it to the east, may have served as a *diakonikon,* or vestry, one of the functions of which was to hold the gifts of the community. In the 5th and 6th centuries after Christ members of the congregation regularly brought to church private offerings of grain, olive oil, and wool as well as the bread and wine used in the celebration of the Eucharist.

The nave of the Basilica was separated from the aisles by rows of columns, most likely five or six to a side, made of drums reused from the interior Corinthian colonnade of the

Temple of Zeus. These columns, as comparison with other basilicas of this date in Greece suggests, would have rested on an elevated stylobate, or line of column bases, while low parapets in the intercolumniations would have prevented any direct circulation between the nave and the aisles. A block, decorated with a large incised cross in a square field, perhaps formed one of these parapets; that block now sits against the stylobate of the northern colonnade not far from the eastern end, facing the nave. Such a barrier both maintained a clear distinction between the clergy performing the service and the communicant but nonparticipant congregation, and kept the nave free of obstructions for the ceremonial processions which still form an important part of the Eastern rite. The congregation was also strictly segregated by sex: in larger, more opulent churches, the women were regularly isolated in galleries built over the aisles and furnished with independent entrances, but at Nemea, as in other small churches, this requirement was probably satisfied simply by placing men and women in separate aisles. (The tradition that assigns men to the right aisle and women to the left, although beginning to die out, continues today in the Orthodox churches of Greece, particularly in rural regions.)

The interior decoration of the Basilica was spare and simple, as befits the parish church of a small agricultural community. No trace of sculptural ornament or mosaic has survived, and the floors were roughly paved with plain terracotta tiles. The walls of the nave and aisles, however, and presumably the narthex as well, were covered with stucco and brightly painted. Pieces of plaster found during excavation preserved clear traces of paint: the color scheme included red and yellow in the nave and (less securely) muted blue in the aisles; the details of the decoration, however, are lost.

At the eastern end of the church, occupying the entire apse and extending some 3.50 m. into the nave, is the *bema,* or sanctuary, which contained the altar table and the *synthronon,* a semicircular podium with seats for the officiating clergy. The *bema* was separated from the nave by a wall or screen, known by a variety of names among the Early Christians and called the *templon* or iconostasis by the later Byzantines. The term *iconostasis* as used today by architectural historians is something of an anachronism in the Early Christian context since the screen in the 5th and 6th centuries was not literally an iconostasis, adorned with painted *eikones,* or portraits, of Christ, the Virgin, and the saints, nor was it usually tall enough to obstruct the congregation's view of the sanctuary and the altar. The typical Early Christian screen was a low parapet, its panels embellished not with portraits but with patterns incorporating the cross and other Christian motifs executed in relief or perforated latticework. Here, in keeping with the available materials and the economy of decoration already observed elsewhere in this Basilica, the screen was constructed of plain blocks of dark blue-gray limestone re-used from an ancient monument. Although they may have carried some modest incised decoration like that on the aisle parapet block mentioned earlier, no ornamented surface has survived. Parts of four parapet blocks are still *in situ* at the eastern end of the nave, two on either side of the central passage through the screen to the *bema,* together with the stump of a column which marked the northern edge of this passage.

Just behind the screen the *bema* is paved with stone apparently taken from the same ancient monument plundered for the parapets. Blocks of blue-gray marble are laid in rows alternating with similar blocks of white limestone. On the surface of some pieces are cuttings for the placement of a sculptural group which seems to have included at least one horse; the structure from which they came (now known as the Nu Structure; see pp. 155–57) was perhaps a victory monument dedicated by the winner of an equestrian event at the games some eight hundred years before the construction of the Basilica. If any of the bronze statuary itself still survived when the base was dismantled, it doubtless went into the furnaces to be melted down along with broken tools, bits of scrap, and clamps pried from the blocks of the Temple, for the Early Christians regarded pagan sculpture with suspicion at best, and metal remained throughout the Middle Ages a scarce and precious material (note the scraps of bronze statuary in museum case 6; see p. 32).

In the center of the *bema* stood the altar, of which nothing has survived; probably, like most Christian altars of this date in Greece, it was a plain rectangular table of marble supported on four legs or small columns. Behind it, in the apse, where there is no stone paving, was the *synthronon*. The construction of this part of the Early Christian *bema* was subject to much regional and individual variation, and its precise form in the Basilica at Nemea is not known.

The roof of the building, as of all Greek basilicas of the 5th and 6th centuries, was made of wood and has consequently perished (except for the hundreds of terracotta tiles which once covered it). There may have been a clerestory above the nave to provide light, but it is perhaps more likely in a Basilica of such restricted means that the only lighting came from windows in the north and south walls, and possibly in the apse as well (as in the basilica on Evangelistria Hill). Tiny fragments of colorless glass which may have come from windowpanes were found in the area during the early excavations.

The main structure of the Basilica was probably built in the late 5th or early 6th century after Christ. Later, though probably not much later, a baptistry was added on the northern side, built up against the north wall of the Basilica and incorporating as part of its west wall the eastern side of the small room north of the narthex. This annex comprised the baptistry proper, to the north, and a narrow room sandwiched between it and the north wall of the church (see Fig. 26). A threshold block in this wall indicates that the narrow room was accessible from the north aisle; presumably it communicated with the rest of the baptistry as well, although no trace of a connecting doorway survives and the northern part of the structure seems to have been provided with an independent outside entrance on the west. The purpose of the narrow room is not clear, but it may have served as a *chrismarion* or *consignatorium,* where the ceremony of confirmation and the ritual anointment of newly baptized Christians took place.

The baptistry proper, a rectangular structure *ca.* 13.00 by 9.50 m., consisted of two parts: an inner chamber, the so-called *photisterion* (*ca.* 6.00 m. square), which contained the font; and a corridor (*ca.* 3.00 m. wide) on three sides of the central chamber. This tetragonal plan with a peripheral corridor is known from other baptistries of the period in Greece, Asia Minor, and elsewhere.[48]

The corridor was paved with terracotta tiles similar in size and appearance to those used in the nave, aisles, and narthex of the Basilica. A low bench *ca.* 0.45 m. wide once ran along the inside of the outer wall except where interrupted on the west, apparently by a door from the outside. (This door was located just west of the conspicuous round hole in the floor of the western corridor, which is a later medieval intrusion unrelated to the baptistry.)

The *photisterion* was separated from the corridor on the west, north, and east by a partition wall of unknown height. Traces of benches similar to those which lined the outer wall were found against the western side of this partition, facing the corridor; they may have continued around to the north and east as well. There was certainly a doorway in the western partition wall, opposite the entrance to the baptistry from

48. These include the baptistries at Eleusis, Kos, Alabanda (in Karia), and Gul-Bakhche (near Smyrna); also very similar is the 6th-century baptistry at Saint-Maurice d'Agaune in Switzerland. For bibliography see I. E. Volanakes, Τὰ παλαιοχριστιανικὰ βαπτιστήρια τῆς Ἑλλάδος (Βιβλ. ᾿Αθ. ᾿Αρχ. ῾Ετ. 84: Athens 1976) 39–41; and A. Khatchatrian, *Les baptistères paleochrétiens: plans, notices et bibliographie* (Paris 1962).

the outside, and probably another on the north; for the eastern side evidence is lacking, but another doorway is not precluded.

Within the area enclosed by the partition the remains of two distinct floor levels are visible, both paved with terracotta tiles larger (*ca.* 0.55 m. square) than those used in the corridor. The earlier pavement is best preserved in the southwestern corner of the chamber; here the tiles are set, like those in the corridor, with their edges more or less parallel to the walls of the building. In the later pavement, visible along the eastern side of the chamber, however, the tiles are laid diagonally. Both pavements are partially preserved in the northwestern corner, where the chronological sequence of the two phases can be made out (the diagonally oriented tiles rest on top of the earlier floor). The change may have been prompted by damage to the original paving caused during repairs to the baptistry plumbing.

In the center of the *photisterion* lies the *kolymbethra*, or baptismal font, a stepped, sunken basin (*ca.* 0.40 m. deep) formed of concrete and originally faced with marble. (The large marble slab found *in situ* in the bottom of the basin was in fact a reused piece of a Christian ritual dining table; see p. 43.) In a later remodeling of the font the two circular steps leading down into the central part of the basin were built up with stone, tile, and concrete approximately to floor level along most of the font's circumference. A circular strip (*ca.* 0.65 m. wide) was cut back into the tile paving around the font, and the entire area was ringed with low parapet blocks, two of which still remain on the north side. Wastewater from the font flowed through a lead pipe to a drain, built of stone, which ran under the northern corridor of the baptistry and emptied into the more western of the two wells just outside the north wall.[49] (The prominent block with a deep "channel"

---

49. The well was out of use by the Early Christian period, but material from its lower levels is displayed on the top shelf of case 9 in the museum; see p. 42.

east of the font should not be mistaken for part of the baptistry plumbing; it is in fact an ancient stele base reused in the
eastern partition wall.)

The basin may seem surprisingly small and shallow, but
baptism in the Early Christian period was regularly performed not by immersion but by affusion: the *catechumen,* or
newly instructed convert, stood in the font while the officiating cleric poured water over his head from a small vessel.[50]
Later, as Christianity grew more pervasive and the baptism
of adults more and more infrequent, large independent baptistries like this became obsolete throughout the Christian
world. They were replaced by small fonts within the church
itself, which proved more convenient for the now-standard
practice of infant baptism.

The baptistry, like the Basilica, was covered with a wooden
roof, which has perished except for the tiles and a handful of
iron nails used in its construction. Fragments of glass in the
destruction debris again suggest the presence of glazed windows for lighting, and traces of red and blue pigment found
on a small chunk of plaster indicate that here too the walls
were stuccoed and painted with bright colors. There is also
evidence that the inner face of the screen wall around the *photisterion* was at least partly decorated with a revetment of
green marble, an unexpected touch of luxury in light of the
paucity of ornament surviving from the Basilica itself.

The Basilica with its baptistry is the most important architectural monument of the Early Christian period at Nemea,
and the only one visible on the site today. It did not stand in
isolation, however, as excavation in the surrounding area has
shown. Contemporary with the baptistry, or perhaps slightly
later, an enclosure was constructed northwest of the Basilica,
incorporating on the southeast the corner formed by the west

---

50. C. F. Rogers, "Baptism and Christian Archaeology," *Studia Biblica et Ec-
clesiastica* 5 (1903) 239–358.

wall of the baptistry and the north wall of the small room north of the narthex. Only small sections of the south and east walls were found during excavation, and the full extent of the enclosure is not known, but it appears to have been an open yard containing, among other things, a cistern and a well (see p. 117), the latter dating back at least to the Hellenistic period but continuing in use, after a long period of abandonment, into the 5th and 6th centuries after Christ.

More substantial were the remains of a large 6th-century house uncovered in the area immediately southwest of the Basilica (Figs. 28 and 29). This complex of rooms, which may represent more than one dwelling, abutted the southwestern corner of the church and extended some 40 m. to the west; other remains of what was probably the same complex were found by excavators in the 1920s in the area between the Bath and the Basilica and above the east room of the Bath itself. The rooms were fairly regular in shape and size at the eastern end but smaller and haphazardly laid out further west, suggesting that the western rooms were later, *ad hoc,* additions built as the complex expanded outward from its original site close to the church.[51] The walls were constructed of plastered mud brick on a socle of unmortared rubble, the roof was wooden with a covering of clay tiles, and the floors, though occasionally paved with tiles or flat stones, more frequently consisted simply of hard-packed earth. The large quantities of coarse household pottery, lamps, fragments of glass goblets, and other similar material recovered from the building leave no doubt about its domestic function, and we may tentatively identify it (or at least part of it) as the residence of the Basilica's clergy. Further excavation below the levels of the Early Christian period has necessitated the re-

51. In spite of this, the ceramic and numismatic evidence suggests that the entire complex had a compressed history, with construction, occupation, and abandonment all taking place over a few decades in the middle and the second half of the 6th century.

Fig. 28. Early Christian house walls immediately southwest of the Basilica, from the southwest.

Fig. 29. Early Christian house walls south of the Bath, from the east.

moval of these remains, but a narrow baulk of earth supporting part of several rubble foundations is still preserved along
the southern scarp of the trench immediately south of the east
room of the Bath.

Apart from architectural remains, the Early Christians left
their mark on the site in two important ways: by farming the
land and by burying their dead around and within the decaying
Sanctuary of Zeus. Neither activity was intentionally destruc-
tive of ancient monuments, and both were necessary, but the
damage they caused has done more to hamper our understanding of the Greek and early Roman periods at Nemea
than even the deliberate dismantling of the Temple and other
ancient structures for building material.

Agriculture has taken the greatest toll. In fairness to the
Christians of the 5th and 6th centuries, however, we should
acknowledge that the Christians of the 12th through the 20th
century are equally culpable: for over fifteen hundred years
the rich soil of the Nemea valley has attracted farmers to
whom, understandably, flourishing crops are more important
than buried and inedible antiquities. Early Christian farming
trenches, which regularly take the form of narrow oblongs
laid out in rows (a photograph of a typical plot is on display
in the museum; see p. 44), have been found throughout the
site, on both sides of the river, except in the immediate vicinity of the Basilica and in the areas set aside as cemeteries.
These trenches were dug with stubborn persistence through
considerable obstacles and partially eradicated the foundations of many ancient buildings. (The softness which made
poros, the light yellow stone often used in foundations, easy
to work also made it particularly vulnerable to later destruction. This is clear, for example, from the remains of several
oikoi; see pp. 124–26.) Even where they did not uproot blocks
and hack through walls, the Early Christians, with their
plows and hoes, churned the distinctly stratified layers of
earth from earlier periods into a homogeneous mass, destroy-

ing the archaeologist's most valuable source of information in reconstructing the history of the site.

Over a hundred Early Christian graves have been excavated at Nemea since the 1920s, some widely scattered, others clustered in cemeteries at the northwestern corner of the Temple, along the river between the Temple and the Bath (especially around Circular Structure A), and southeast of the Basilica. The number is uncertain because the similarity of medieval burials and the absence of grave goods make 5th- and 6th-century graves difficult to distinguish from those of the later Byzantine and Frankish periods, especially in contexts disturbed by later agricultural activity. The graves vary from simple earth burials to more elaborate constructions of tile and stone; in the most common Early Christian type the floor and walls of the grave were lined with roof tiles, while additional tiles formed a cover. A characteristic example of a more solidly constructed medieval grave is located near the steps to the Basilica (see p. 78).

The simplicity of these burials and the relative scarcity of personal effects interred with the remains testify once again to the poverty of the Early Christian settlement at Nemea. Most of the graves excavated to date contained nothing but the bones of the deceased; a few have produced rings, small crosses, belt buckles and, in one case, a handful of iron tacks from a pair of hobnail boots, the organic parts of which had long since disintegrated. The large quantity of jewelry and the cosmetic items found in one young woman's grave near the Temple of Zeus (see Fig. 13 and the discussion at museum case 11, p. 45) mark that burial as exceptionally lavish by local standards and suggest that she belonged to an important family in the community.

Although never wealthy, the Early Christian community seems to have been most prosperous in the second half of the 6th century after Christ; numismatic evidence in the excavated area increases for this period, and there are signs of rapid growth and expansion.[52] Just at this point, however, the settlement was suddenly and completely abandoned: the archaeological record breaks off abruptly, and with the exception of a few stray coins probably dropped by passing travelers, there is no trace of activity on the site for the next five hundred years.

The abandonment is not hard to explain. In the 580s after Christ the defenses of the Isthmos were breached and the Peloponnesos finally overwhelmed by a great influx of Slavic tribes, one of several waves which swept down along the Balkan peninsula from the regions north of the Danube during the 6th and early 7th centuries.[53] Evidence of violent destruction from the nearby sites of Corinth, Kenchreai, Argos, and Halieis (Porto Cheli), along with that from Athens and other sites outside the Peloponnesos, can be firmly dated to the mid-580s; contemporary chroniclers as well as Slavic pottery discovered in the destruction debris at Argos identify the agents of this catastrophe beyond doubt.[54]

At Nemea most of the Christian inhabitants seem to have fled before the invaders arrived. The housing complex southwest of the Basilica showed no signs of violent destruction (in

52. See preceding note.

53. The literature on the Avaro-Slavic invasion of Greece is extensive and often bitterly controversial. For recent summaries of the literary and archaeological evidence, together with useful bibliographies, see P. Yannopoulos, "La pénétration slave à Argos," in *Etudes argiennes* (*BCH* suppl. 6: Paris 1980) 323–72; and M. M. Weithmann, *Die slavische Bevölkerung auf der griechischen Halbinsel* (*Beiträge zur Kenntnis Südosteuropas und des Nahen Orients 31:* Munich 1978).

54. Kenchreai: R. Hohlfelder, "A Small Deposit of Bronze Coins from Kenchreai," *Hesperia* 39 (1970) 68–72, "A Sixth Century Hoard from Kenchreai," *Hesperia* 42 (1973) 89–101, and "Migratory Peoples' Incursions into Central Greece in the Late Sixth Century: New Evidence from Kenchreai," *Actes du XIVe congrès international des études byzantines, 1971* (Bucharest 1975), III, 333–38 (= "Barbarian Incursions into Central Greece in the Sixth Century of the Christian Era: More Evidence from Corinthia," *East European Quarterly* 9 [1975] 251–58); R. Scranton, "The Harbor-Side Sanctuaries," in R. Scranton, J. Shaw, and L. Ibrahim, *Kenchreai I, Topography and Architecture* (Leiden 1978) 67–68. Argos: P. Yannopoulos, *op. cit.* (n. 53); and P. Aupert, *BCH* 107 (1983) 851–53. Halieis: W. W. Rudolph, "Excavations at Porto Cheli and Vicinity. Preliminary

fact it apparently stood vacant until the roof fell in from dis-
repair), but the large quantity of pottery and the many coins
left behind suggest a hasty departure. For those who chose
not to flee the prospects were grim: a small excavation con-
ducted in 1974 some 500 m. south of the sanctuary uncovered
the ruins of another house destroyed at the same date, with
the scattered remains of its inhabitants strewn across the floor.
No doubt a Christian or Christians from the settlement, fear-
ing the threat of such violence, took refuge in the partly silted-
up entrance tunnel of the Stadium, hoping to hide unnoticed
until the danger was past (see museum, p. 47, and Stadium,
pp. 188–90).

In some communities disrupted by the Slavic incursions,
life continued, if only temporarily and with much-reduced
resources. Nemea, however, never recovered. The Slavs did
not settle in the vicinity themselves, and the Christian inhabitants who fled and survived apparently made no attempt to
return to their homes. The Nemea valley remained deserted
for half a millennium.

Renewed human activity on the site began in the 12th and
13th centuries after Christ when another agricultural community grew up among the ruins of the ancient sanctuary.
The life of these Byzantine farmers probably differed little

Report V: The Early Byzantine Remains," *Hesperia* 48 (1979) 294–320. The
situations at Corinth and Athens are somewhat more complicated and the pub-
lications more widely scattered. For Corinth see the references in Yannopoulos,
353–57. (The most important articles are now outdated, however, and the interpretation of destruction layers must account for earthquakes as well as invasion; a
new survey of this period in Corinthian history is badly needed.) For Athens
D. M. Metcalf, "The Slavonic Threat to Greece *ca.* 580: Some Evidence from
Athens," *Hesperia* 31 (1962) 14–23, provides a good introduction, with additions
by, e.g., J. H. Kroll, G. C. Miles, and Stella G. Miller, "An Early Byzantine and
a Late Turkish Hoard," *Hesperia* 42 (1973) 301–9; and T. L. Shear, Jr., "The
Athenian Agora: Excavations of 1972," *Hesperia* 42 (1973) 395–96. Coin hoards
from the Peloponnesos of the 6th and 7th centuries, useful in pinpointing the
date of the incursions, have been collected by A. Avramea, "Νομισματικοὶ
'θησαυροὶ' καὶ μεμονωμένα νομίσματα ἀπὸ τὴν Πελοπόννησο," Σύμμεικτα
5 (1983) 49–90.

from that of their Early Christian predecessors, and in fact the physical remains of the two communities are similar, consisting largely of plow furrows, irrigation ditches, and the omnipresent graves. Traces of buildings and cisterns have been discovered within the sanctuary, and some rooms added onto the northern side of the Basilica date from this period, although it seems unlikely that much of the old church was refurbished, considering the number of medieval graves found within its walls. The digging of these graves, which range from small private burials to enormous ossuaries, destroyed much of the Basilica's tile paving and must postdate the use of the building as a place of worship.

The site continued to be used, at least as a burial ground, throughout the later Middle Ages. Graves of Frankish and early Turkish date were found south of the mound formed by the dilapidated ruins of the Early Christian Basilica, on top of which, sometime during this period, a small chapel was constructed of ancient material now reused for the second or third time. (This chapel, itself in ruins, remained partly standing as late as the nineteenth century, by which time popular imagination had already labeled the mound the "Tomb of Opheltes"; see Fig. 2.) With the gradual blocking of the outlet of the Nemea River, however, the valley floor became marshy and inhospitable, and once again the site was given over to "the dreary vacancy of death-like solitude" Dodwell (see n. 11) found here in 1805, which prevailed until the restoration of proper drainage in 1883 and the foundation soon after of the modern village of Herakleion, now Archaia Nemea (see p. 10).

The Xenon I

The visitor standing in the 6th-century Basilica simultaneously stands in a building of the 4th century B.C., one-third of which is covered by the Basilica. Labeled Xenon on the plan

(Fig. 30), this more ancient building probably served as a hotel for some of the athletes and trainers who came to Nemea every two years to compete in the Panhellenic games.

Hotels were ubiquitous in ancient Greece by the 4th century B.C.,[55] but few scholars have investigated the physical evidence and the written sources which pertain to them.[56] Thucydides—the only ancient author to mention the architecture of a hotel—laconically described one built at Plataia in 426 B.C. as measuring 200 feet on each side with rooms all around, above and below.[57] This description has been interpreted as that of a square building with a central court and has been used to identify some buildings with such a plan as hotels. The building at Nemea, however, differs from Thucydides' description. Rather than being square, the Xenon here is a long, narrow rectangle which clearly lacked a central court. Indeed, for its time, the Xenon's plan was unique. It has been possible, however, to identify it by using criteria of location, plan, and associated finds.

Eating and drinking vessels as well as hearths for cooking found throughout the southern rooms indicate that these rooms were restaurants of a sort; the paucity of such evidence in the northern rooms suggests that they were used for living and sleeping. The plan of the building, which was divided into apartments, with sleeping quarters and dining areas in each, further suggests that it can be identified as a hotel, or *xenon*. The location of the Xenon, near the Sanctuary of Zeus but outside the Sacred Square, on the major road through the

55. Buildings to provide temporary shelter for visitors seem to have been typical at the larger sanctuaries of antiquity: at Olympia the Leonidaion and at Epidauros the *katagogeion,* for example.

56. Greek hotels are mentioned briefly in general books such as L. Casson, *Travel in the Ancient World* (Toronto 1974), and specific examples are discussed in some guidebooks to sites or in individual articles. The only complete exploration of the subject is by L. Kraynak, *Hostelries of Ancient Greece* (Ph.D. diss., University of California, Berkeley, 1984).

57. Thucydides 3.68.3.

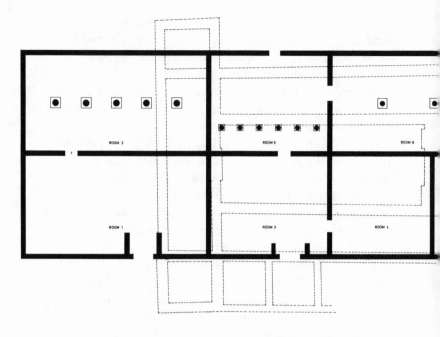

valley, suggests that the structure was secular but played an important role in the business of Nemea; its proximity to the Bath brings it into the realm of athletics. Finally, excavations in Room 12 produced a jumping weight, and *strigils* have been found elsewhere. Thus this was not only a *xenon* but specifically a building designed to house the athletes who came from all over the Greek world to compete at Nemea.

The Xenon is visible where it emerges east and west from beneath the remains of the Basilica; it extends for a total of 85 m. A median wall divides the structure longitudinally; latitudinal walls form rooms of varying sizes. The Xenon, like the Temple of Zeus, has *parastades,* or walls which project into the rooms on either side of the five doorways in the south wall along the main road. Projections like these in the

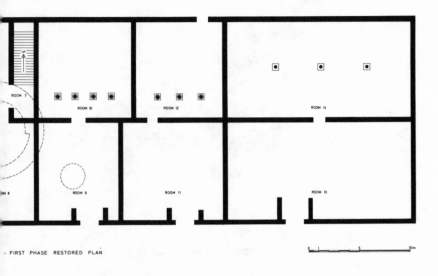

Fig. 30. Restored plan of the Xenon with outline of the Basilica.

Temple on either side of the cella door protected delicate
moldings from damage, but there was no similar need in the
Xenon. The two doorways found in the north wall lack projections like those beside the doors in the south wall. But even
though the reason for them remains obscure, the projections
serve us well by marking the facade of the Xenon; the building was oriented toward the ancient road, not the sanctuary.

Another odd feature of the Xenon is the row of interior
columns in all but one of the northern rooms. Although interior columns *per se* are common enough, the position of these
in the Xenon, some on the longitudinal axis of a room, others
south of it, is unusual. Inasmuch as the columns must have
served to support weight, and since they occur only in the
northern rooms, a second story has been restored over the

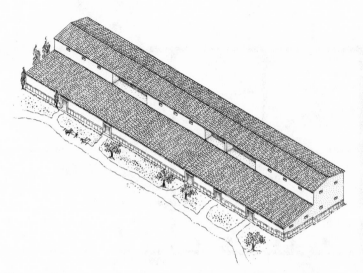

Fig. 31. Perspective drawing of Xenon with restored second story and roofs.

northern part of the building (Fig. 31). The rooms restored above Rooms 5, 10, and 12 have recessed balconies whose back (north) walls are supported directly by the off-center columns of the ground-level rooms. The anomalous shape of Room 7 is due to its use as a stairwell giving access to the second story.

The western end of the Xenon protrudes from below the narthex of the Basilica. Only the foundations of the exterior walls and column bases in Room 2 remain. The median wall of the Xenon protrudes from beneath the nave of the Basilica, crosses the narthex, and continues outside it. In this wall, built of reused blocks of all sizes and shapes, "mortared" with clay, the Aristis inscription now on display in the museum (see p. 37, Fig. 11) was found reused.

Several trenches (now backfilled) have been sunk through the tile pavement of the narthex. At the bottom of one trench the continuation of the median wall of the Xenon is visible

and, north of it, a square column base which is the easternmost base in Room 2. A coin of Philip II found in this portion
of the median wall verified that the Xenon was built in the
late 4th century B.C.

The median wall of the Xenon continues uncovered for the
entire length of the nave, disappearing into an undug portion
before reappearing in the apse of the Basilica. Although the
remains of the Xenon within the nave appear chaotic and confusing at first glance, they are worth exploring.

East of the threshold at the entrance to the nave and north
of the median Xenon wall are six column bases, one with the
stub of a column still *in situ* (in Room 5 on the plan). Although originally discovered long ago, the record was so
sketchy that it could not be understood until old trenches
were cleared in 1980. The rediscovery of these column bases
was especially welcome because Room 5 had been the only
major northern room which seemed to lack interior columns.
Moreover, the column stub gives us the type and diameter of
the columns in this room, evidence not available for other
colonnaded rooms.

A scrappy, poorly constructed wall which crosses the median wall of the Xenon and touches the corner of the second
column base from the northwestern corner of the nave represents a second, hastily built, phase of the Xenon, documented
elsewhere in the remains. The occasion for it was the brief period around 235 B.C. when Aratos of Sikyon returned the
games to Nemea (see museum case 18, pp. 57–58, and n. 35).

The visitor can obtain a closer view of the median wall
from the unexcavated strip of ground along the south side of
the nave whence more of the excavated portion of the Xenon
is visible. Here, in the corner of Room 4 formed by the median wall and the wall between Rooms 3 and 4, is a round
hearth paved with cobblestones. When it was discovered in
1962, a stand like that in House 4 (see p. 76), roughly made of
reused roof tiles to support a pot over hot coals, was found

Fig. 32. Hearth and stand in the northwestern corner of Room 4 of the Xenon in 1964, from the south. The stand has since been removed.

over the northeastern part of the hearth (Fig. 32). The hearth itself was covered with ashes, several pots (shattered when the roof collapsed), and cow bones (one cleaved by a sharp instrument). Clearly Room 4 was a kitchen. The food prepared there may have been consumed in Room 3, on the other side of the wall from the hearth, where a group of drinking cups and cooking pots was found, pressed into the dirt floor when the wall and roof fell on them.

Beyond the hearth (to the east) another scrappy wall crosses the median wall of the Xenon and disappears into the scarp. The date of this wall corresponds to that of the other poorly built wall near the base of the column in Room 2; it too represents Aratos's short sojourn in Nemea.

The visitor who returns to the south aisle of the Basilica can visit the eastern end of the nave for a view of the apse and

Fig. 33. The apse of the Basilica, with the eastern end of the Xenon visible in the background, from the west.

the area beyond it (Fig. 33). The median wall of the Xenon continues into the apse with the threshold between Rooms 6 and 8 and, beside it, another reused block, set in upside down, with the inscription Telestas, a man's name.[58]

After a tour of the rest of the site, we shall return to the eastern end of the Xenon, where the remains allow us to see how the building was constructed. For now, however, we return down the steps from the Basilica to the path, turning right (west) along the path over the ancient road. We leave the path where it turns north toward the Temple of Zeus, striking out westward along the line of a modern road which crosses a bridge over the Nemea River. Just to the right (north) of a large service gate in the fence is the Heroön.

58. IG IV.486. The letter forms suggest a date in the 5th century B.C.; the man Telestas whose name is inscribed here should not be confused with the one whose name is scratched on the Stadium tunnel wall (see pp. 36 and 188).

The Heroön

Excavation of the Heroön took place in 1979, 1980, and 1983. The area had been greatly disturbed by agricultural activity in the Early Christian period and later; the effects can still be seen in the foundation stones scarred by plowing.

Three phases of construction can be distinguished in the Heroön: early Archaic, late Archaic, and early Hellenistic.

THE HELLENISTIC STRUCTURE

The early Hellenistic phase is the one most visible today (Fig. 34). This latest structure took the shape of a lopsided pentagon, its outline possibly influenced by construction here during the late Archaic period. The south and east walls were set at right angles, more or less, to each other. The north and west walls were set at oblique angles, with a change in direction at the southern end of the west wall.

The north wall is just over 30 m. long and has four buttresses at intervals along its interior face. The east wall was originally 22.35 m. in length, but more than half of it was destroyed long ago by a shift in the course of the Nemea River. Ironically, the southern portion of the east wall is the best-preserved part of the Heroön, with five of the original reddish limestone orthostates still in position. The dimensions of the orthostates average 0.48 by 0.92 m., with a height of about 0.50 m. The south wall, slightly more than 36.50 m. long, has four interior buttresses. The west wall heads north for 4.50 m., then veers northeast for 25.50 m. to join the north wall. There were also four interior buttresses for the west wall.

For the most part, only the foundations of the Hellenistic Heroön are still extant. These are cut from a soft yellow poros, a malleable stone which deteriorates quickly when exposed to the elements. The average foundation block is 0.65

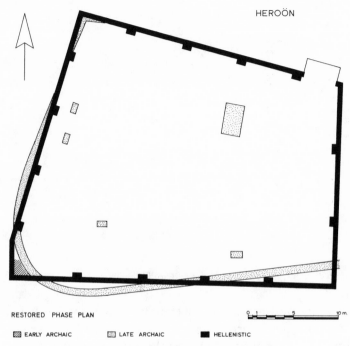

HEROÖN

RESTORED PHASE PLAN

0 1   5   10 m.

▨ EARLY ARCHAIC   ▨ LATE ARCHAIC   ■ HELLENISTIC

Fig. 34. Plan of the Heroön, with phases.

by 1.25 m. At fairly regular intervals, blocks made of this
same material project inward from the wall foundations, apparently as underpinnings for buttresses or the like. The actual wall above the foundations was no thicker than 0.50 m.
to judge from robbing trenches and the next higher course of
orthostates preserved at the southeastern corner of the
enclosure.

The foundations supported a high fence, probably of stone,
rather than a structural wall. The Heroön seems to have been
unroofed; no interior roof supports have been found, and
such supports would have been needed in such a large building. The structure is also strangely shaped to accommodate
conventional roofing. In addition, there is some evidence for

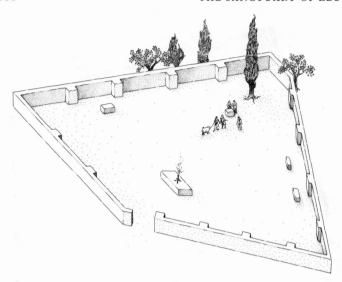

Fig. 35. Perspective view of the restored Heroön from the northeast.

trees having grown inside the Heroön, so perhaps we should
think of a fence surrounding a grassy, sylvan area. Several
stone blocks firmly positioned in the open area of the Heroön
should perhaps be identified as individual altars (Fig. 35).
This matches Pausanias's description of altars and the tomb of
Opheltes within the enclosure. The tomb itself might have
been a construction northeast of the center of the enclosure.
Although now little more than a small, roughly aligned enclosure surrounded by fallen stones, this was once a rectangular structure measuring about 1.40 by 3.15 m. It was erected
as part of the late Archaic phase and may have continued in
use during the 4th century and following, perhaps function-
ing much as did the so-called Leokorion in the Athenian
Agora.[59]

59. See the description and references given in H. A. Thompson, ed., *The
Athenian Agora* (Athens 1976) 87–90.

The entrance to the Heroön was at the northeastern corner facing the Temple of Zeus, where poorly preserved foundations for a monumental porch or gate stand outside the north wall. Measuring approximately 1.00 by 4.50 m., this porch was perhaps roofed over with curved Lakonian tiles, many small fragments of which were found at this place.

The area of the enclosure seems to have been cleared and leveled for a new construction phase in the late 4th or early 3rd century B.C. Traces of the ritual inauguration of the renovated shrine can be seen in the burial of a pot against the north wall and its easternmost buttress. When excavated, this vessel contained a greasy, dark brown earth. This may once have been the pulse (boiled beans) and vegetables inside what Aristophanes described as installation or dedication pots (see museum case 4, p. 28, and n. 24). The Hellenistic chronology of the Heroön's latest phase makes the enclosure roughly contemporary with the new construction of the Temple of Zeus and the other post-Classical building activity at Nemea.

THE LATE ARCHAIC STRUCTURE

The strange shape of the Hellenistic building may be due to the irregular dimensions of the late Archaic construction since the foundations of this earlier building provided additional support for the 3rd-century structure. This sequence is particularly clear on the western side of the building where the rubble courses of the Archaic phase more or less underlie the Hellenistic ones. The two walls diverge slightly in the southwestern corner, with the earlier wall forming a curve instead of an actual corner (Fig. 36).

Other traces of the late Archaic enclosure have been uncovered beneath and perpendicular to the preserved portion of the Hellenistic east wall near its southern end. The foundations of this enclosure, formed of two courses of unshaped

rough stones, were considerably less formal than those of the
later phase. They may have supported a mud-brick wall, protected on top by the tiles found in excavation. As yet no
evidence for doors or gates has been uncovered. Although
greater chronological precision is not possible, this phase can
be dated to the second half of the 6th century B.C.

Inside the late Archaic Heroön was the rectangular structure made of large boulders placed on edge (see p. 106). The
large amounts of ash, bone, and apparently votive deposits
associated with this structure suggest cult activity—possibly
an altar or, as already suggested, the tomb of Opheltes.[60]

THE EARLY ARCHAIC STRUCTURE

Remains of a yet earlier Archaic phase (in the first half of the
6th century B.C.) can best be seen in the southwestern corner
of the enclosure, where stone foundations of ashlar masonry
are cut by, and therefore predate, the curvilinear rubble wall
of late Archaic construction. Other features that may be connected with this phase lie further north along the west wall. A
jumbled mass of rocks near the midpoint of the wall may have
been left over from the dismantling of the early wall, then
used as packing for later landscaping. More of these large
unworked stones lie under the northwestern corner of the
Heroön.

There is a sharp contrast between the cut poros foundation
blocks from the southwestern corner and the unaligned, unworked stones to the north. What sort of activity took place
here during the early Archaic period? Were there two different structures? Was the same function involved? The present

---

60. This is not to say that an actual burial was located here; rather, it was a
legendary one; no evidence of human burial has been uncovered at the Heroön.
Such cenotaphs were common in antiquity, e.g., the "Tomb of Achilles" at Elis
attested by Pausanias 6.23.3 and 24.1.

Fig. 36. Aerial view of the Heroön, 1980.

state of the evidence does not allow us to answer these questions easily.

The early Archaic phase can be dated to the first half of the 6th century, around the time traditionally given for the establishment of Nemea as a site for Panhellenic athletic contests. Apparently the earliest "Heroön" had been in existence for about fifty years when the late Archaic enclosure was constructed.

Pausanias described the Heroön of Opheltes near the Temple of Zeus at Nemea as a θριγκὸς λίθων, "fence of stones," surrounding the tomb of the child. He used this particular phrase in four other instances, including his accounts of the shrines of Ino-Leukothea at Megara and of Pelops at Olympia.[61] The Pelopion has been excavated, and the information thus gained has been useful in reconstructing the Heroön at Nemea.[62] The function of the two structures, after all, was the same: to monumentalize and sanctify the tomb of a dead hero.

The identification of this area as the hero shrine of Opheltes has already been discussed (pp. 27–29). Although the Pelopion at Olympia occupies a central location in the sanctuary near the Temple of Zeus, here at Nemea the shrine to the hero whose mythical death is central to the foundation story of the games lies on the periphery of the Sanctuary of Zeus. The topography thus illustrates and emphasizes the extent to which Zeus dominated the games, the sanctuary, and the baby-hero. Nonetheless, the scale of the Heroön and the quantity of the dedications discovered within it show that the cult of Opheltes enjoyed a fair popularity.

The Bath

Returning to the flagstone path, we notice the southwestern corner of the Xenon to our right; south of it and along the edge of a gravel surface of the ancient road runs a section of the terracotta aqueduct which brought water to the Bath. This simple aqueduct was constructed of U-shaped tiles, curvilinear inside, rectilinear outside. Covering the channel

61. See Pausanias 2.15.3 for his description of the Heroön at Nemea; 1.42.8 for Ino-Leukothea; 5.13.1 for Pelops. Further comparison of these sites is invited by similarities in myth. Ino-Leukothea is identified as the mother of Melikertes-Palaimon, the hero of the Isthmian Games. The other two sites are also chthonic sanctuaries, i.e., the sanctuary of Chthonia at Hermione (2.35) and the sanctuary of the Mistress near Akakesion (8.37).

62. See A. Mallwitz, *Olympia und seine Bauten* (Munich 1972) 133–38.

formed by these tiles were ordinary roof tiles, most frequently (as here) rectilinear, peaked Corinthian cover tiles
(Fig. 37) but occasionally curvilinear Lakonian cover tiles or
even flat pan tiles, apparently used in making repairs. East of
the Basilica and beyond the modern cemetery, in the middle
distance, is a ravine the floor of which has been leveled by
modern agricultural activities. To the right (south) of this is a
large modern reservoir and immediately beside it a Turkish
fountain house (Fig. 37, at arrow). At one time these were
fed, like the aqueduct for the Bath in its time, by a copious
spring near the head of the ravine. That spring was tapped by
a tunnel with a vaulted ceiling cut back some 16.40 m. into
the bedrock (Fig. 38). Although its date has not been established, this tunnel would have been appropriate to the creation of the Bath.

From the flagstone path, with the Xenon to the east and
the Bath to the west, we can see that the two structures are
precisely the same width and have the same alignment. These
similarities suggest that they were a part of the same building
program, and excavations have shown that the aqueduct for
the Bath is only slightly later than the Xenon.

Visitors enter the Bath by way of the large East Room
(nearly 20 m. square) in the center of which are the foundations for four interior roof supports which form a smaller
square (Fig. 39). The southeastern foundation retains its base
(a large weathered gray block); the other foundations are preserved only far below the level of the original floor. During
the Early Christian period this area was dug down some 0.40
m. below the level of the original floor; for this reason no evidence for the location of ancient doors has survived.

The West Room of the building consists of another large
space divided into three east-west aisles by two rows of columns. In the northern row four of the five original bases remain; the central one was destroyed when the Nemea River
forced its way through the building in early modern times.

Fig. 37. The aqueduct from the west, with Corinthian cover tiles in the foreground; the arrow shows the region of the spring on the eastern side of the valley.

Fig. 38. View of the rock-cut tunnel for the spring.

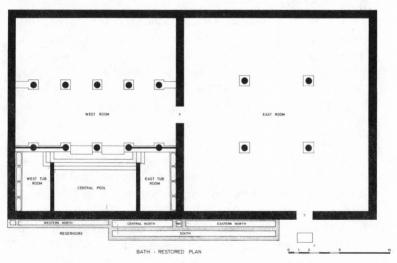

BATH - RESTORED PLAN

Fig. 39. Restored plan of the Bath.

The rerouting of the river to its present course (very close to its ancient bed) took place only in 1924, after the Bath had been discovered.

The south aisle of the West Room is actually a sunken bathing chamber. The columns dividing it from the rest of the room (the bases of only the three furthest east are now visible) are actually projections from the line of the wall marking the limits of this bathing chamber. This chamber is approached from the middle aisle of the West Room through the intercolumniations to the right and left of the center column, beyond which a broad staircase leads downward. The Doric capital in the museum courtyard (A 7; see p. 73), discovered at the western end of this staircase, provides important details for the reconstruction of the interior colonnade. The intercolumniations flanking the two at the center were blocked by a parapet over the sunken chamber to prevent accidents; several blocks of that parapet have been reerected in something like their original positions.

The bathing chamber is itself divided into three parts, all of which exhibit heavy coats (in some areas two layers thick) of hydraulic cement. The wide Central Pool is separated from the smaller flanking rooms by a wall which was about chest high originally, as is indicated by a socket cut into the south wall (Fig. 40). The flanking rooms are virtual mirror images of one another. Each was entered by the side steps of the staircase, and each is equipped with four stone tubs placed end to end along its rear wall. These tubs were fed by a stone water channel set back into the wall; it was pierced at appropriate intervals by holes through which the water flowed into the individual tubs.

Although two tubs have V-shaped notches in their sides for overflow, none of the tubs is equipped with an outlet. Notches cut at the top of their common walls allowed water to flow from one tub to another. Wastewater in the East Tub Room flowed across the floor to an opening at the corner of the staircase. A terracotta channel under the staircase, behind its

Fig. 40. View of the bathing chamber from the north.

first step, carried the water to the opposite corner of the staircase, where it simply flowed out over the floor of the West
Tub Room to a hole beneath the northernmost tub. This, in
turn, connected with the Nemea River. Wastewater from the
West Tub Room itself flowed to the same hole, whereas that
of the Central Pool ran into a hole at its own northwestern
corner to join the channel beneath the staircase; from there it
flowed through the same system as the wastewater of the East
Tub Room. For the wastewater system to work, the floors of
the rooms had to be progressively lower toward the west.[63]

A hole in the south, or back, wall of the Central Pool
marks the entry point for its water; its height shows that the
water in this pool would have been about chest high or slightly
lower and that the pool itself was intended as a plunge bath.
The tubs in the flanking rooms were too shallow and short to

63. The hole at the base of the north wall of the West Tub Room and the
cement channel set into the ancient floor leading to it are not ancient but were
created in 1958 by N. Verdelis of the Archaeological Service.

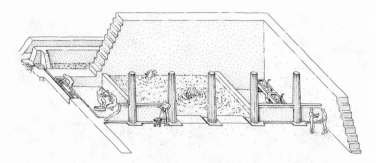

Fig. 41. Restored perspective of the bathing chamber.

be individual bathing tubs. Ancient representations show clearly that they were meant to be used as basins from which to splash or throw water on the body (Fig. 41).

Parts of the reservoir system that supplied water are visible from the southwestern corner of the East Room. These would have been fed by the aqueduct, but the remains at the point of connection have been obliterated. Nonetheless, the general workings are clear. Two long narrow reservoirs, originally about 1.00 m. deep and 0.60 m. wide, run alongside the exterior south wall of the building. The one closer to the building is interrupted just at the southeastern corner of the East Tub Room where a smaller tank, a 0.60 m. square "water closet," is formed. Both the larger and the smaller reservoirs served only the East Tub Room, and the existence of the water closet shows that the flow of water was not constant but rather was regulated by periodic flushings of the water closet.

The reservoir west of the water closet and the entire southern reservoir served the Central Pool and the West Tub Room. Whereas probably the pool was completely filled and emptied at intervals of several days, the West Tub Room would have been regulated in the same manner as the East Tub Room. Unfortunately the reservoirs west of the inlet to the Central Pool are not preserved, so that the details of operation are not certain.

The Bath, firmly dated to the last third of the 4th century B.C., is one of the earliest bathing systems known in the Greek world. More difficult than dating, however, is the assignment of a precise ancient name. At an athletic center like Nemea we would expect a *palaistra-gymnasion* complex, and the *palaistrai* of Delphi and Olympia, to cite the most relevant examples, were equipped with bathing facilities.[64] They seem, however, to be a generation or so later than the example at Nemea. Moreover, the Nemea structure, although sizable, does not have all the subsidiary rooms (for boxing, oiling, etc.) we expect in a *palaistra,* nor does it have the practice running tracks, approximately 200 m. long, always found in a *gymnasion.* At Delphi and Olympia such tracks are obviously present, but at Nemea there is no space available for them in association with the Bath.

Without evidence for the ancient name,[65] it seems best to refer to the building as a bath and to leave open questions about the restriction of its use to athletes.[66]

The Oikoi I

To the right of the flagstone path, north of the Xenon and the Bath, is a large square block, reused in the Early Christian period as a wellhead (see p. 90). Discovered broken into four

64. See Mallwitz, *op. cit.* (n. 62) 278–89 for the *palaistra-gymnasion* complex at Olympia, and J. Jannoray, *Fouilles de Delphes,* II, *Le Gymnase* (Paris 1953) for Delphi. Very recent excavations in the *xystos,* or covered race track, in the Delphi *gymnasion* have revealed more of its features and parts of a victors' list of the Roman era; see *BCH,* Chronique 111 (1987) 609–12.

65. The circular altar dedicated to "Zeus in the Grain Office" (I 9 in the museum courtyard; see p. 72 and n. 40) was perhaps discovered immediately south of the Bath. It is difficult to see any connection between the Bath and a grain office—whatever that might be.

66. For bathing establishments and customs in the Greek world see R. Ginouvès, *Balaneutiké* (Paris 1962). Although Ginouvès's subject goes beyond that of this survey, none of the examples he collected serves as a precise architectural parallel for the Nemea Bath.

pieces and thrown down the well, the head has been mended
and reestablished in its original position (although it had an
even earlier life, as shown by the *anathyrosis* on its sides). At
each corner of its upper surface shallow depressions show
where vessels were placed while water was fetched. The well,
which extends slightly more than 10 m. below this stone
head, may originally have served Oikos 1, which lies directly
north (Fig. 42).

The scanty remains of two walls east and south of the well
may have formed part of a back room for Oikos 1 by analogy
with the rooms behind Oikoi 8 and 9 (see pp. 165–67). Beyond these walls, extending under the northwestern corner of
the baptistry of the Basilica, was a pit filled with marble
working chips and tools (see museum case 20) used to manufacture the sima for the Temple of Zeus in the later 4th century B.C.

Oikos 1 (across the path from a circular foundation to
which we shall return) is the first of the nine *oikoi* which extend eastward from the flagstone path.

Oikoi is the plural form of the Greek word *oikos*, meaning
"house" but also used to denote tent, room, chamber, estate,
and birdcage.[67] As an architectural unit an *oikos* has no fixed
features; the word is used generally to describe a building set
up within a sanctuary by a city-state. Although the precise
use of the building is uncertain, it may have served more than
one purpose—as a combined treasury and meeting hall, for
example. Although the first *oikos* in the series at Nemea was
discovered in the 1920s and the first two *oikoi* as well as the
northwestern corner of the third were explored in 1964, the
buildings were not identified as *oikoi* until the whole series
was uncovered during the 1970s. At that time it was possible
to see that they formed a unit related to this site as the treasuries of Olympia were related to theirs.[68] The Nemean *oikoi*,
like the treasuries at Olympia, are similar buildings in a line

67. *LSJ*⁹ (1940) *s.v.* οἶκος.
68. See Mallwitz, *op. cit.* (n. 62), 163–79.

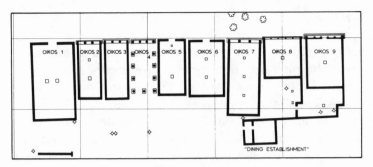

Fig. 42. Plan of the row of *oikoi*.

defining one boundary of the sacred area of the sanctuary. Simple architecturally, the *oikoi*, like the Olympian treasuries, were meant to be impressive only from the front facing the square, in this orientation proclaiming to visitors the wealth of the city-state which had erected each one. Thus it is tempting to connect two reused blocks found in 1964, one inscribed "of the Rhodians" (I 105; see p. 70) and the other "of the Epidaurians" (I 31; see pp. 71 and 169), with the *oikoi* and to suggest that they identified one *oikos* as that of the Rhodians, another as that of the Epidaurians.

Despite their similarities to the Olympian treasuries, the Nemean *oikoi* are much larger (at least four of the Nemean *oikoi* are larger than the largest Olympian treasury). In addition, no dedications (which one would expect to find in a treasury) survive in connection with the Nemean *oikoi*, perhaps because the buildings are poorly preserved, extensive farming activity in the Early Christian period having obliterated the floor levels of many of them. Perhaps a closer analogy can be made with the *oikoi* at Delos, a series of buildings, comparable in size to those at Nemea, which lie along a curve at the northern boundary of the sanctuary of Apollo.[69] These

69. The size of the Nemean *oikoi* and the absence of a *prodromos*, or antechamber, which is a part of the Delian *oikoi*, of the majority of the Delphian treasuries, and of the Olympian treasuries, may suggest the form of a large, simple lesche. See J. Pouilloux, *Fouilles de Delphes*, II, *Topographie et Architecture, La region nord du sanctuaire* (Paris 1960) 132, n. 3.

buildings, which may have been used for meetings and ritual
banquets,[70] housed offerings and diverse material, including,
according to the inventory inscriptions cataloguing their contents, libation bowls, iron anchors, bronze pins, tripods, oak
timber, bronze lamps, incense, bronze rams' horns, ships'
beams, and all varieties of pottery.[71] Thus it might be appropriate to think of the Nemean *oikoi* as storerooms, embassies,
or meeting halls and not simply as treasuries. In fact, although there is only comparative evidence that the Nemean
oikoi were used as treasuries, there is positive evidence that
they had some unique uses, which will be discussed as we
consider each building individually.

Because the *oikoi* are poorly preserved, their history cannot be easily traced. Oikoi 4, 5, and 6 were constructed in the
first half of the 5th century B.C., and although Oikoi 2 and 3
cannot be definitely dated, there is no evidence that they
could not also have been constructed at that time. Moreover,
since Oikoi 2 through 6 are built on the same level and planned
with roughly the same dimensions, it seems probable that
they were constructed at the same time. Oikoi 1 and 7, unlike
the others, are slightly out of alignment; their deviation—one
slants to the southeast, the other to the southwest—may only
reflect the importance of the facade: the buildings were perhaps not meant to be scrutinized from various vantage points.
Therefore we can probably assume that the *oikoi* were all built
at roughly the same time in the first half of the 5th century
B.C. There is evidence that many of them were either destroyed or had been remodeled by the late 4th century B.C.
Those which survived were robbed out by later inhabitants of
the site, and all suffered extensive damage from farming
activity.

70. For more on *oikoi* see P. Bruneau and J. Ducat, *Guide de Délos* (Paris
1983) 120.
71. See, e.g., *Inscriptions de Délos* (Paris 1926) nos. 180, 296, 298, 300,
and 442.

OIKOS I

The largest of the series, Oikos I measures 22.40 by 13.15 m. (on average). Its floor level has been lost because of the extensive farming by Early Christians in this area, and the building is preserved almost exclusively in its soft yellow poros foundations, which are themselves often missing or eroding because of exposure. When the building was in use, these blocks would not have been exposed to the air. The entire foundation of the south wall is missing except for one block in the southwestern corner which allows us to establish the dimensions of the building. The only blocks preserved above the foundations are those at the northeastern corner, the eastern interior base visible just east of the center of the *oikos,* and the remnants of a second base 2.00 m. west of the first. These two column bases could have efficiently supported the entire roof. Although no other *oikos* has this exact plan, the *oikoi* are all of a type: a simple rectangular shape, with roof supports sufficient for the size of the building provided where necessary.

In 1977 the area west of Oikos I was explored to uncover any further *oikoi* in this direction. Although no further buildings were uncovered, the area was found to consist of compact layers of earth, suggesting the existence of an ancient path to the Temple beside Oikos I, roughly in line with the modern flagstone path.

Beyond the west wall of Oikos I lies a curious row of unworked stones set into the earth. Each stone is pierced by a hole formed naturally when water eroded away the larger stones of the conglomerate rock. The stones seem to have been chosen because of these holes and placed so that the holes were just above ground level. They are level with the top of the poros foundations and are all perpendicular to the west wall. Only six stones remain *in situ,* although seventeen were noted during the 1926 excavations, including one cylindrical worked poros stone. No satisfactory explanation of their function has been offered; perhaps they were used to hold ropes used as anchors or tethers. Subsequent excavations uncovered similar stones in several other *oikoi*.

North of the north wall of Oikos 1, two more inset stones are visible, the one further west pierced like the others, the one further east unpierced. These stones flank the area of the main doorway, evidenced by a second foundation block representing a threshold abutting the southern side of the north wall, visible south of and in line with the unpierced stone. The size and nature of this entrance cannot be precisely determined because an Early Christian grave cuts through this southern block and its immediate neighbors in the north wall.

OIKOS 2

The northern foundations of Oikos 2, east of Oikos 1, consist of a double rather than a single row of poros stones. Although nothing remains above them, the extra reinforcement indicates that they supported a heavy and ornate facade which faced onto the Sacred Square. Moreover, the northern foundations of Oikos 2 protrude slightly beyond the line of the side walls, and the building narrows 0.20 m. from north to south, further emphasizing its northern orientation. It seems likely that the purpose of the double-width foundation and its extension beyond the side walls was to accommodate the *krepidoma,* or three-stepped platform, of a columnar or pseudo-columnar facade, with setbacks for one or two steps. The similar doubling of the northern foundations on Oikoi 3, 4, and 7 indicates that these *oikoi* probably had similarly ornate facades. An example of this sort of facade is shown in the reconstructed drawing of Oikos 9, whose northern foundation was similarly doubled and extended but whose facade was reconstructed based on more specific evidence (see Fig. 60, p. 165). Oikoi 1, 5, and 6 probably had simple facades since they do not have a double northern foundation.

Fig. 43. Interior column base with pierced stones in Oikos 2, from the north.

The two interior column bases for Oikos 2 can be seen along its north–south axis. The northern base rests partly on a reused hard limestone *euthynteria,* or leveling course, block to the north and a poros block to the south. The surface of the *euthynteria* block has been worked down in the southern center section to receive the base, and the block still shows a well-preserved molding on its northern edge. Another poros stone to the south, flanking the poros stone on which the base partially rests, serves no apparent function in the present arrangement. The northern base appears originally to have been 0.50 m. further south; if this is the case, the bases would have been equidistant from each other and from the north and south walls.

Four more of the naturally pierced stones observed along the west wall of Oikos 1 can be seen in a line between the two interior bases of Oikos 2 (Fig. 43), and a fifth is visible just south of the southern base. The holes piercing these stones

are not oriented uniformly like those of the stones along
Oikos 1; instead, some are parallel to the walls, some perpendicular to them. These stones can be positively associated
with the occupation of the building; any explanation of their
function and that of the stones along Oikos 1 must be plau-
sible in both an indoor and an outdoor context.

OIKOS 3

The most striking feature of Oikos 3 is the trench, dug in the
1920s, which runs through the center of the building along its
north-south axis. Part of the northwestern corner of this *oikos*
is also cut by a 1964 trench, visible in the northeastern corner
of Oikos 2. Nothing remains above the foundations of Oikos
3, and there are no traces of its interior supports or its south
wall. The protrusion of the facade foundations beyond the
side walls is more pronounced in Oikos 3 than in Oikos 2,
but in general this badly damaged *oikos* is similar to Oikos 2.
The east wall of Oikos 2 and the facing west wall of Oikos 3
show that the buildings are aligned with each other.

OIKOS 4

The next *oikos* to the east, Oikos 4, was a building with col-
onnades on all four sides. The fragmented remains of four
column-support bases approximately 3.50 m. apart on centers can be seen in place of east and west walls. The base in the
southwestern corner is the best preserved; from it the approximate dimensions of 1.20 by 1.00 m. for the bases are ob-
tained. A few stone fragments midway between the remains
of this block and those of its western counterpart may represent a center column-support base. If so, it would establish
the southern boundary of the building. The hard limestone
block south of the southeastern base does not appear to be
part of this structure. Three more of the naturally pierced

stones can be seen between the southeastern and central bases, all with holes oriented east–west and none definitely associated with the occupation of the building. One hard limestone block at the western end of the facade lies lengthwise abutting the double row of poros blocks; it is not answered by a similar block on the eastern end. This block may indicate the need for added reinforcement at this point. The square area cut down to a lower level in the northeastern corner of this *oikos* is the remnant of a 1920s trench.

OIKOS 5

East of Oikos 4, Oikos 5 is one of the best-preserved *oikoi* despite the robbing out of its north wall, perhaps late in the 4th century B.C. The rest of the foundations are well preserved except for those in the southeastern corner, where a Byzantine pit cuts through both these foundations and a large section of those in the southwestern corner of Oikos 6. A 1920s trench also cuts through the northeastern section of the building, just inside the east wall. The rubble socle of the upper wall can still be seen atop the southern and southwestern foundations. Midway along the south wall are two adjacent reused limestone blocks larger than those elsewhere in the rubble of the upper wall. The western block displays a dowel cutting in the center of its upper surface and a posthole cutting for a doorpost in its northwestern corner, both from its previous context; the eastern block has a pair of "ice-tong" lifting holes from its previous use in the Early Temple. A shallow ledge cut into the rocks approximately 0.10 m. from the edge runs along the western and northern sides of the western block and the northern and eastern sides of the eastern block. These cuttings for a doorstop and pivot hole show that these blocks, as reused, formed the threshold of a single-leaved door approximately 0.95 m. wide. This door dates from a period later than that of the original construction of the *oikos,* probably the late 5th or early 4th century B.C., as indicated by the stratigraphy south of the doorway.

Of the two interior bases in Oikos 5, the southern one (0.75 by 0.85 m.) is more than twice the size of the small northern one (0.50 by 0.55 m.). The great distance (8.70 m.) between these bases relative to the 16.10 m. overall north-south length of the *oikos* implies that a third base was located between the existing two. Just to the west, along the same axis as these bases, are seventeen pierced stones similar to those found in or near the other *oikoi.* Here the stones can definitely be associated with the period when the *oikos* was occupied. The holes in the stones have no apparent consistent or meaningful orientation, and the number of holes in each stone varies, some having two or three but most having one, 0.03 or 0.04 m. in diameter. The reddish pigment in several of these stones may be related to their function but may also be due to natural causes.

This *oikos* had a short but active history. Constructed, like the others, in the first half of the 5th century B.C., it suffered an initial destruction in the second half of that century and a secondary destruction during the late 2nd century B.C. The inside of the building shows signs of three periods of occupation: the first corresponds to the laying of the foundations and the placement of the pierced stones. The second, now visible, accumulated after these elements were in place; the southern interior column base was placed atop this layer, and the holes of the pierced stones, still exposed, could have been used during this second period as well. In the third period, at the end of the 5th or beginning of the 4th century B.C., the back doorway was added. Large quantities of lead and of iron finds and marble chips churned up by Early Christian farming in this area suggest that a period of industrial activity on the site followed the destruction of the building. Most of this material was found where the line of pierced stones has been broken through, suggesting that the stones were out of use when the industrial activity took place.

OIKOS 6

More conventional than Oikos 5, Oikos 6 displays two interior bases, dividing its north-south length of just over 16 m. into regular intervals of 5.10 m. Although this *oikos* also dates from the first half of the 5th century B.C., there is ceramic evidence of earlier activity on the site as well as evidence that the building was either destroyed or heavily remodeled in the mid 4th century B.C.

Despite their similarities, Oikoi 1 through 6 (and 7 as well) seem to have functioned as discrete units. The history of Oikoi 8 and 9 differs from that of both the other *oikoi* and any other *oikoi* or treasuries known from antiquity, as we shall see when we return to these structures after visiting the Temple and the Sacred Square.

Sacred Square I

Now we retrace our steps to the flagstone walkway to examine the foundation of a circular structure opposite the *oikoi*.

CIRCULAR STRUCTURE A

More than thirty blocks of hard limestone, variously shaped, lie in patchwork fashion in two irregular concentric circles with two stones in the center. The entire foundation measures approximately 6 m. across; in the center, an area about 5 m. in diameter has been dressed down to receive an upper course of stones. The small cuttings for prying these missing stones into place, visible on the tops of the stones in this dressed-down part, indicate that one or two concentric rows of stones were fitted here. It is not known whether the resulting central space, about 2.50 m. in diameter, was left empty or filled with rubble or stones.

The area around this monument was disturbed in Early Christian times. Little evidence exists to place the circular structure in the history of the sanctuary. It seems to have been built in the second quarter of the 5th century B.C. or somewhat later. Pottery and a coin from Phlious in the material from its destruction indicate that it probably survived only until the end of the 5th century or the beginning of the 4th. It was destroyed violently, for crushed and decayed stone was found mixed in the soil just over and beside the preserved foundation.

The discovery of tiny pieces of bronze in association with the destruction of the monument suggests that the foundations supported a statue (on a two- or three-stepped base, perhaps), but we have no idea of the subject. The solid course of foundations may have been intended to provide a firm base for a valued work of art.

THE EARLY WALL

Again on the path to the Temple of Zeus, we can see on the right two ancient wellheads, side by side. The contents of these wells are in the museum, cases 10 and 18 (see pp. 44 and 54–58).

The remains of a rubble wall left of the path and parallel to it are surely a remnant of the Archaic sanctuary, built before the end of the 6th century B.C. The position of this wall at the western end of the Temple may be significant; the sunken crypt of the Temple, at a similar level, is perhaps an indication that an especially sacred spot, important for the Archaic sanctuary, has been preserved.

Although the wall itself has an early date, the block at its northern end (reused from the Early Temple of Zeus) rests on construction debris of the 4th-century Temple. It must have been put in place near the end of the 4th century B.C. at the earliest. A pair of rectangular cuttings in the top of this stone matches another pair in a block at the southwestern corner of the Temple foundations, suggesting that the stones were part of a gateway or barrier at an oblique angle to the southwestern corner of the Temple. This possibility, however, is complicated by another pair of cuttings on the western side of the same corner block of the Temple and by similar pairs of cuttings at the northeastern and northwestern corners of the Temple foundations. No traces of a wall exist at either of these corners; however, another single reused block from the Early Temple lies off the western end of the Temple's northwestern corner. If this block formed the end of a wall, it would have run east–west instead of north–south. At the northeastern corner, the situation is even less clear; the cuttings in two reworked blocks may correspond to those in the stones at the western end of the Temple.

If indeed these cuttings are for gateways, the system enclosing the northern and western sides of the Temple must have been important in the sanctuary. Limited excavation, however, has produced practically no evidence for construction of any sort in these areas, although two limestone blocks about halfway along the western end of the Temple and a little more than 2 m. west of the Temple may once have supported a dedication or small altar. We might conclude that the location of the wall at the southwestern corner of the Temple is coincidental and that the cuttings and individual blocks are associated in some way with the construction of the Temple.

The Temple of Zeus

The flagstone path ends at the southwestern corner of the Temple of Zeus, and the visitor ascends the ancient foundations at this point. A good vantage point for the following discussion is the line of the west wall of the Temple's cella, north of the large orthostates.

HISTORY

The Temple of Zeus was constructed during the last third of the 4th century B.C. (*ca.* 330) as part of an extensive building program throughout the sanctuary. Its predecessor, the Early Temple, had been constructed early in the 6th century B.C. and destroyed more than a century later. The violence of that destruction is shown clearly by the heavy deposit of ash and carbon amid the debris; the large quantities of melted and fragmentary bronze, including many arrowheads; and the badly burnt architectural elements (see museum case 19, pp. 58–61). The builders of the 4th-century Temple dismantled and reused blocks belonging to the earlier structure when setting the foundations for the later building.

The complex of kilns to the south, in the area east of the Basilica (see museum case 20, pp. 63–67) is associated with the 4th-century Temple. In these kilns, used in the latter part of the 4th century (as attested by ceramic and numismatic evidence) for the manufacture of roof tiles, were found tiles whose fabric, size, and design match those found within the Temple. The evidence of the kilns confirms nicely the construction date assigned to the Temple on stylistic grounds.

Evidence for the destruction of the Temple is less clear. By the 2nd century after Christ the roof had fallen in, and the cult statue was gone (Pausanias 2.15.2). That the main structure remained standing is demonstrated by the stylobate of the cella, where surface weathering indicates that the interior Corinthian order stood exposed for a significant time. (The circular surface of the stone around the square *empolion* cuttings had been protected by the standing Corinthian columns and thus remains relatively smooth.) How the Temple came to its present state of ruin is difficult to determine. It appears that the destruction was gradual, caused to a great extent by human intervention. Earthquakes, including two major ones in the late 4th century after Christ, may well have caused serious damage to the Temple, but by no means can they account for its complete destruction. The absence of most of the *krepidoma* can be explained only by the robbing out of the blocks. The two surviving stylobate blocks show clearly that the columns fell when the stylobate was cut away. One block, at the third column from the northwestern corner on the north side, whose original side surfaces have not been preserved, shows traces of deliberate cutting. The other block, that supporting the standing peristyle column, has been cut at the northeast, and the lowest drum of the column above this block is cut at the southwest as if in preparation for "felling" it. The columns appear to have fallen at different times, most during the 5th and 6th centuries after Christ, but some as late as the 13th century.[72]

The Early Christians actively quarried the Temple when constructing their Basilica (see pp. 79, 80, 82, 83–84), extracting, principally from the interior, such material as cella wall blocks and parts of the Corinthian colonnade. A large pit dug in the 5th or 6th century after Christ just south of the Temple, filled with roof tiles as well as nails and assorted fragments of Temple blocks, probably represents the cleanup work following (or accompanying) the sorting and removal of material for use in the Basilica.

THE EARLY TEMPLE OF ZEUS

The 4th-century Temple has all but obliterated its predecessor, and it is very difficult to reconstruct the plan and design of the Early Temple from its few surviving elements. At the northern end of the crypt, at the rear (western end) of the 4th-century Temple, a segment of foundation wall of the Early Temple can be seen. It extends from the east wall of the crypt below the stairs to the west wall. This wall, which probably

72. S. G. Miller, "Poseidon at Nemea," *ΦΙΛΙΑ ΕΠΗ* I (Festsch. Mylonas, Athens 1986) 261–71.

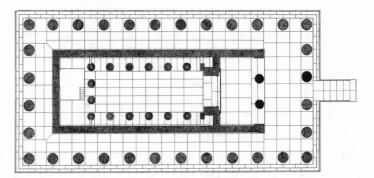

Fig. 44. Restored plan of the Temple of Zeus, after B. H. Hill, *The Temple of Zeus at Nemea* (Princeton 1966), Pl. IV.

represents the southern limit of the Early Temple near its western end, shows that the two buildings were oriented on different but parallel longitudinal axes. The width of the wall suggests that it did not support a multistepped *krepidoma*. This evidence, added to that provided by the only surviving elements of the superstructure—wall and pavement blocks, some of which may be seen off the northwestern corner of the 4th-century Temple—confirms that the Early Temple did not have a surrounding colonnade. It did have a hipped roof of Corinthian tiles decorated with a series of impressed antefixes and palmette-shaped ridge akroteria. (The architectural material of the Early Temple is discussed on pp. 58–61.)

THE 4TH-CENTURY TEMPLE OF ZEUS

The 4th-century Temple (Figs. 44 and 45) used three architectural orders: an exterior Doric peristyle and an interior Corinthian colonnade which was topped by a second story of the Ionic order. It had a pronaos *in antis,* or porch with facade columns framed by *antae,* and, in keeping with a tendency of 4th-century building, omitted the *opisthodomos,* or rear

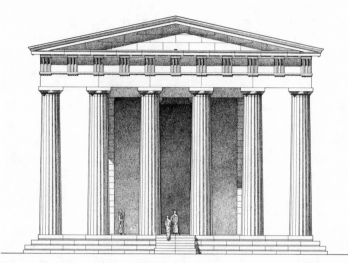

Fig. 45. Restored eastern facade of the Temple of Zeus, from Hill, *The Temple of Zeus at Nemea*, Pl. VI.

porch. At the rear of the cella, in place of the *opisthodomos,* was an *adyton* (the innermost room of a temple which was "not to be entered": we might say "the holy of holies").[73] Another characteristic of its age is the shortened plan with six columns across the facade and twelve along the sides as opposed to the Classical proportion of six by thirteen. The crypt within the *adyton* is an unusual feature. The finished building contained no sculpted decoration. Although conservative in design, the Temple shows great care and precision in execution and, in several instances, interesting solutions to structural problems.

Building Materials. Most of the stone used in the 4th-century Temple is limestone, certainly quarried from the low

73. For omission of the *opisthodomos* in the 4th century, see G. Roux, *L'archi-tecture de l'Argolide aux IVe et IIIe siècles avant J.-C.* (= *BEFAR* 199, Paris 1961) 328; for the *adyton* at Bassae, *ibid.* 52–55; for the *adyton* at Delphi, G. Roux, *Delphes: Son oracle et ses dieux* (Paris 1976) 101–17.

ridge running along the eastern side of the valley between
Nemea and Kleonai (see p. 10). Although the stone has become hard and gray from exposure and weathering, when
first cut it is actually soft and sandy reddish limestone. Blocks
of the same limestone from the Early Temple were reused
along with newly quarried stone in the foundations of the
4th-century Temple. Newly quarried blocks were used in the
superstructure. Black marble was used for the threshold of
the cella door.[74] Soft limestone was used in the interior for the
Corinthian capitals of the lower order and for the Ionic upper
order. This stone is easier to carve, and within the cella it
would not have suffered from exposure to the elements. The
limestone was coated with a fine white stucco, which served
both to protect exposed surfaces and to decorate the stone.
Traces of blue and red decoration appear as well.[75] White Pentelic marble was used for the sima (a typical feature in 4th-
century architecture of the Argolid).[76] The roof was constructed of wooden rafters over which terracotta roof tiles of
local manufacture were layered.

Foundations and Krepidoma. The *krepidoma* and its foundations (Fig. 46) may best be viewed at the northwest. The
foundation blocks of the peristyle continue for seven courses
(2.80 m.) below the *euthynteria.* A series of parallel foundation walls, three or four courses deep, supports the interior
paving. The north–south orientation of these walls in the
cella is visible where the paving is broken away; in the pro-

74. Some of the threshold blocks were removed from their original position
sometime between 1915 and 1924 (see Clemmensen and Vallois, *op. cit.* [n. 13]
1–20, Pls. I–II and Fig. 5, where the southern portion of the threshold was apparently still *in situ*). The stone is similar to that employed in the Tholos at Epidauros, which is referred to as "black Argive stone" in the building accounts
there (*IG* IV² 103.15).

75. These traces occur on triglyphs (blue) and metopes (red); on one of the
cornice blocks, where the mutules are blue and the fascia red; and on the plastered surface of the underside cyma reversa molding, where fine incised lines indicate that it carried a painted Lesbian leaf decoration.

76. Roux, *L'architecture, op. cit.* (n. 73) 328.

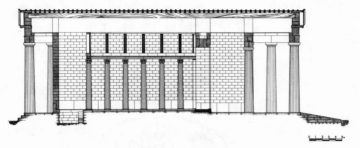

Fig. 46. Restored longitudinal section of the Temple, from Hill, *The Temple of Zeus at Nemea*, Pl. VIII.

naos and the crypt the walls run east–west. The space between them was originally packed with earth and construction debris such as stone chips.

Building Techniques. The Temple measures 20.09 by 42.55 m. at the stylobate level. Squared blocks laid next to and on top of one another in typical Greek fashion are held together, if at all, by iron clamps and dowels. These iron clamps, of a hook type with lengths ranging from 0.30 to 0.40 m., were sealed into their cuttings with molten lead, which prevented air and moisture from rusting the iron and which acted also as a cushion to absorb shock and to provide a certain flexibility. Few examples of either clamps or dowels remain because the demand for iron and lead during the Early Christian and later periods claimed most of them. Two clamps, however, may be seen at the center of the western end of the Temple, and a fragment of an iron dowel with some of its lead is in the museum (IL 236; see case 20, p. 67).

Although the vertical joining surfaces of blocks were treated with *anathyrosis,* hard and soft pockets in the limestone made the working of perfectly smooth surfaces difficult. To obtain the tightest fit possible, a saw was run through the joining surfaces between blocks so that they would mirror each other. Traces of saw marks are visible on several blocks.

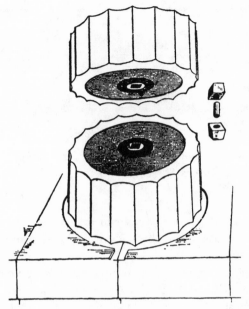

Fig. 47.   An empolion.

Column drums were aligned by means of *empolia*, the square cuttings for which are visible in many fallen drums around the site. A pair of wooden blocks inserted at the center of each column drum held a rounded wooden centering peg (Fig. 47). The peg ensured the proper alignment of column drums but was not important structurally.

The Temple platform exhibits horizontal curvature, which is known in other ancient Greek temples.[77] At Nemea the center of the platform on the long sides is nearly 0.06 m. higher

77. Virtually imperceptible deflections from true horizontal or vertical lines have been identified in Greek architecture and various explanations offered for them; they are interpreted either as errors in modern observation and calculation or as intentional measures to correct optical illusions which were expected to arise otherwise. See F. C. Penrose, *An Investigation of the Principles of Athenian Architecture* (London 1888) 22–24, 27–35, 36–44; and J. J. Coulton, *Greek Architects at Work* (Ithaca 1977) 108–12.

Fig. 48. Restored Corinthian capital, from Hill
The Temple of Zeus at Nemea, Pl. XXIII.

than the corners. To prevent rainwater from collecting, the
Temple platform slopes down gently from the walls of the
cella.

Cella. The interior colonnade of the cella (see Fig. 46) was
two tiered, running parallel with the north and south walls
and returning across the western end. The lower order was
Corinthian, the upper Ionic (see p. 71). The primary function
of the superimposed columns was probably to help support
the roof, for no evidence suggests that a gallery ever existed.

The free-standing CORINTHIAN COLONNADE had six columns along the sides and four across the western end. The
columns, each composed of five drums, rose to a height of
7.49 m. including capital and base. The capitals (Fig. 48; see
museum A 16, 18, 20, pp. 18, 71) are similar to those at

Tegea.[78] The surface of each capital designed to face the wall of the cella was executed less carefully than the others. The joint surfaces of the column drums are smooth (without *anathyrosis;* the same is true of the exterior columns), and several bear traces of saw marks (see p. 135). The column drums have *empolion* cuttings similar to those found on the top surfaces of the Doric capitals, apparently used in both cases in the rotation of the blocks on a lathe during trimming and carving. (See museum A 138, discussed on p. 72, for an unfinished column shaft clearly worked on a lathe.)

The shafts of two columns have rectangular cuttings for tenons, which may have been used to secure metal screens. The position of the cuttings indicates that the screens rose to at least half the height of the shaft. The screens were probably placed between the columns at the rear (west) of the cella where they would restrict access to the *adyton.* The openings between the corner columns and the cella walls were probably closed with narrow but solid walls, as suggested by a "peninsula" which extends the smooth area of the paving surface from beneath the column to the wall.

The IONIC UPPER ORDER followed the plan of the lower order on whose epistyle it rested. It was composed of a series of quarter- and half-round column shafts carved on the corners and the ends, respectively, of rectangular piers (see museum A 11 and 248, p. 71). The quarter-round columns were placed at the corners, the half-round columns along the sides of the colonnade and probably across the western end, each one centered over the columns of the lower order. The volutes of the capitals were carved with deep grooves, the edges spiraling to terminate in eyes projecting from the capital (Fig. 49). This design would have made the most of the little light entering the upper part of the cella.

78. Roux, *L'architecture, op. cit.* (n. 73) 362–68.

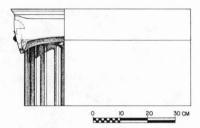

Fig. 49. Restored Ionic capital, from Hill, *The Temple of Zeus at Nemea*, Pl. XXVI.

The WALLS of the cella and pronaos were composed of a *toichobate* (wall base) course raised 0.08–0.09 m. above the peristyle paving and 0.05 m. above the paving of the sides of the cella; orthostate blocks (some still *in situ* around the cella); *plinthoi* (rectangular blocks, many of them reused in the Basilica); and an *epikranitis* (a wall-crowning block with decorative molding) which rested on top. The interior orthostates of the cella walls were set higher (0.43 m.) than the exterior orthostates, corresponding to the different heights of the cella floor and the exterior peristyle floor. The exterior orthostates at both western corners were L-shaped, as were the wall blocks which rested on them. The last wall block placed in each course (i.e., the "center" block) had two parallel rows of horizontal slots resembling ladders cut at each end (Fig. 50). The block would have been lowered with crowbars cutting by cutting and fitted into place.

At the east wall of the cella on either side of the door were *parastades,* or wall returns, projecting over 2 m. into the cella. A pier attached to the western face of each *parastade* formed the eastern end of the interior Corinthian colonnade. The opening for the door between the *parastades* is 4.16 m. wide. When the door, built of two wooden leaves, was opened, each leaf folded against its *parastade*. The *parastade* thus prevented the door from swinging too far back and protected the

Fig. 50. "Center" wall block with horizontal lifting slots.

interior colonnade from such swinging. Similar *parastades*
were used in the Xenon (see p. 98), and the technique is
found elsewhere as well (e.g., at Tegea and Bassae).[79] The design at Nemea, unlike those at Tegea and Bassae, effectively
coordinated *parastade* and interior colonnade.

The CRYPT at the rear (western end) of the cella is rectangular in plan (*ca.* 3.65 by 4.35 m.), with its four walls carelessly
constructed of numerous reused blocks. The poor quality of
the masonry suggests that the walls were faced with either
stucco or stone veneer, although there is no evidence for either. At the eastern side, from the north, six steps (0.71 m.
wide) descended into the crypt to a depth of nearly 2 m. The
lowest three steps are preserved, the top two of which were

79. For *parastades* at Bassae, see Roux, *L'architecture, op. cit.* (n. 73) Pl. I; for
those at Tegea, see C. Dugas, J. Berchmans, and M. Clemmensen, *Le sanctuaire
d'Aléa Athéna à Tégée* (Paris 1924) Pls. IX–XI, LXIII; see also IG II² 1668.23–26
and 59, and the discussion of the term *metopa* in L. D. Caskey, G. P. Stevens, and
J. M. Paton, *The Erechtheum* (Cambridge, Mass. 1927) 304–5.

carved out of a single block. A foundation wall of the Early Temple runs from below the steps toward the west wall of the crypt (see pp. 131–32). The crypt floor was paved with a thin (0.02 m.) layer of cement plaster which rests against the early foundation wall. On the interior faces of the two orthostate blocks of the cella wall immediately west of and above the crypt a curious raised panel has been carved, one not found on any other orthostate blocks.[80]

The function of the crypt remains a mystery. We may suppose that it enclosed an area of some religious significance. Where sunken *adyta* are preserved or recorded elsewhere, they are often associated with oracles (e.g., Temple of Apollo at Delphi).[81] The association of the seer Amphiaraos, one of the Seven who witnessed the death of Opheltes, with nearby Phlious (Pausanias 2.13.7), although suggestive, cannot be considered evidence for an oracular cult at Nemea, which is, moreover, conspicuously absent from the literary sources.[82]

No fragments of the CULT STATUE, already missing when Pausanias (2.15.3) visited the Temple in the mid 2nd century after Christ, have survived. It was probably located in front of the western columns of the cella. In the sanctuary of Nemean Zeus at Argos, Pausanias (2.20.3) saw a bronze statue of Zeus which he attributed to the sculptor Lysippos of Sikyon, who was active in the latter part of the 4th century B.C.[83] It is

80. See B. H. Hill, *The Temple of Zeus at Nemea* (Princeton 1966) 27–29, for discussion of both the northern limit of the crypt and the panels on the orthostates.

81. Roux, *Delphes, op. cit.* (n. 73) 101–17.

82. See L. Bacchielli, "L'adyton del Tempio di Zeus a Nemea," *RendLinc* ser. 8: 37 (1982) 219–37, for an interesting recent study suggesting that the crypt at Nemea was intended for oracular purposes.

83. Cf. Argive coins of Imperial times depicting a standing Zeus, nude, holding a scepter in his right hand, with an eagle at his feet; the type persists virtually unchanged through several reigns and is thought to represent a copy of the statue by Lysippos; F. Imhoof-Blumer and P. Gardner, "Numismatic Commentary on Pausanias," *JHS* 6 (1885) 85, Pl. K: XXVIII.

tempting to suppose that this statue had been removed from Nemea to Argos when the games were transferred there (see p. 57).

The two Doric columns of the PRONAOS remain where they were placed more than two millennia ago, still supporting epistyle and frieze blocks (see Figs. 45 and 46). The columns, made up of twelve drums, are 9.55 m. high. The central epistyle blocks (parallel exterior and interior) are those preserved *in situ*. Contrary to the Peloponnesian tradition, the triglyph-metope frieze of the pronaos was undecorated (i.e., neither sculpted nor painted).[84] The extant frieze includes one block carrying a single triglyph and metope and the central block carrying a single metope (the last block to be placed; see the discussion of the exterior frieze, p. 139).

Exterior Colonnade. The DORIC COLONNADE (see Figs. 45 and 46) consisted of twelve columns along the flanks and six at the ends. Of these thirty-two columns a single example remains standing east of the southern pronaos column. Thirteen drums made up each column, which rose to a height of 10.33 m. The columns are noted for their slender proportions, a feature of late Doric buildings.[85] The column drums display a slight convexity (*entasis*) in their taper, perhaps to correct the optical illusion of a concave outline which would be formed by a shaft with a straight upward taper (see n. 77). The shafts were carved with twenty flutes separated by sharp

84. Roux, *L'architecture, op. cit.* (n. 73) 404.
85. The proportion of column height to diameter is 6.34 to 1 and shows the tendency of the Doric column to grow taller and thinner over the ages. The 6th-century B.C. Temple of Apollo at Corinth, for example, has an analogous proportion of 4.15 to 1. By the 5th century the proportion of column height to diameter on the Parthenon in Athens had become 5.48 to 1. The thin proportions at Nemea have long been noticed by, *inter alios,* W. M. Leake, *Travels in the Morea* III (London 1830) 332: "The slenderness of the columns is particularly remarkable, after viewing those of Corinth; it is curious that the shortest and longest specimens, in proportion to their diameter, of any existing Doric columns, should be found so near to one another. The columns of Nemea are more than six diameters high, or as slender as some examples of the Ionic. . . ."

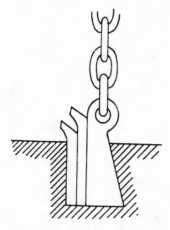

Fig. 51. A lewis: a device inserted into a hole in the upper surface of a stone block so that the block can be lifted without damage to its finished exterior surfaces.

arrises. The lower side of the bottom column drums follows the gentle convex curve and slope of the stylobate.

The EPISTYLE blocks, each 3.75 m. long and paired back-to-back, spanned the distance from the center of one column to the center of the next. At the four corners of the building the interior epistyle had its corner joints cut at 45-degree angles.

The regular unit of the triglyph-metope FRIEZE contains a single triglyph and metope. The arrangement of alternating triglyphs and metopes and the centering of every other triglyph over a column required certain variations to the standard block (e.g., the corner block consisted of two triglyphs and an intermediate metope on its long face and a single triglyph on its short face). The block used near the center of both the flanks and the ends of the Temple consisted of a single metope; this type was the last frieze block to be lowered into place on each side of the building, and it alone shows a lewis hole (seen in cross section, with a lewis inserted, in Fig. 51), used for lifting and lowering.

The frieze backers were designed to rest against the frieze course and to support a peristyle ceiling. The preserved top surfaces, however, show no traces of a ceiling.

The CORNICE rested on and projected over the frieze course. The cornice blocks preserve two cuttings, which were used to secure the wooden rafters of the roof (Fig. 52): sockets were cut on the flat top surface of the blocks along the back edge and shallow depressions along the front edge with cuttings for long rectangular dowels. The bed of the socket is horizontal and does not follow the angle of the pitch of the roof. Thus it is unlikely that it held the sloping rafter. The combination of socket and dowel suggests the use of horizontal tie beams or ceiling joists (set into the socket) to restrain the ends of the rafters (doweled into the upper section).[86]

The austerity of the Doric entablature was tempered by the elaborately decorated marble SIMA (gutter) along its eaves (Fig. 53). Each block of the marble sima is symmetrically designed around a central lion's head spout (used to throw rainwater clear of the building) and ends with a spiraling acanthus tendril (see museum A 3, 5 a–e, 6, p. 71). All the decoration is carved on the vertical face of the block; the bottom edge has a projecting fascia. The lack of a crowning molding on the sima is an Argive and Corinthian detail.[87] Palmette antefixes, also of marble, were placed into cuttings at the joints between sima blocks. The sima supported the tile roofing by serving as a brake against the gravitational force exerted by the tiles. Each unit spanned the width of two pan tiles and had at its center a marble cover tile (actually the continuation of the back of the palmette antefix). Because neither corner nor apex

86. Cornice blocks from Tegea appear to preserve identical cuttings. C. Dugas restores a rafter with a V-shaped end set into the socket and doweled: *op. cit.* (n. 79) Pl. XLIV. Cf. A. T. Hodge, *The Woodwork of Greek Roofs* (Cambridge 1960) 84–85. Hill and Williams's restoration of a horizontal tie beam seems the more likely interpretation of these unusual cuttings (which apparently do not occur elsewhere): Hill, *op. cit.* (n. 80) 15–16.

87. Hill, *op. cit.* (n. 80) 19, n. 48; Roux, *L'architecture, op. cit.* (n. 73) 329.

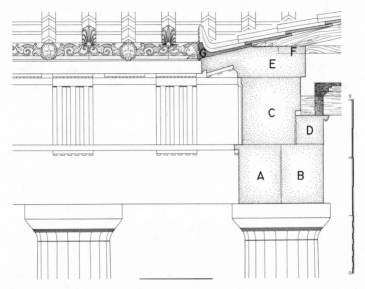

Fig. 52. Restored drawing of the exterior superstructure, from Hill, *The Temple of Zeus at Nemea,* Pl. XIII: A = epistyle, B = interior epistyle, C = triglyph-metope frieze, D = frieze backer, E = cornice, F = horizontal joist socket, G = sima.

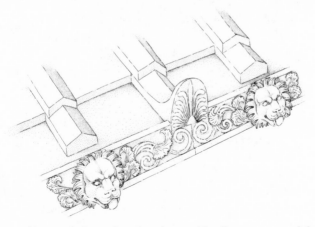

Fig. 53. Restored sima, showing the marble tile stops carved from the same block.

sima blocks (these would have carried cuttings for akroteria bases if they existed) have survived, akroteria cannot be restored.

The PEDIMENTS (see Fig. 45), 17.92 m. long and 1.87 m. high at the center, consisted of three courses over 1.00 m. thick. No conclusive evidence for pedimental sculpture exists.

Wood construction between the rafters and the ROOF tiles is hypothesized on the basis of an inscription from the second half of the 4th century describing the arsenal of Philo in the Piraeus.[88] There, lath and boards held with iron nails and a covering layer were used as a bed for Corinthian tiles.

Corinthian terracotta tiles manufactured in the kilns south of Oikoi 6 and 7 were laid above this hypothetical wooden system for the roof of the Temple of Zeus at Nemea (see p. 168).

The entrance RAMP (see Figs. 45 and 46) at the eastern end of the Temple was built after the *krepidoma* had been completed and met the top of the stylobate in a flush joint (as suggested by the incline of the surviving blocks). Characteristically temples of the Hellenistic period have such ramps; the Temple of Zeus at Nemea is the first of them.

Tegea and Nemea. Several striking parallels between the Temple of Zeus at Nemea and the Temple of Athena Alea at Tegea have been noted. Scholars have suggested that the design of both the sima and the Corinthian capital at Nemea were copied directly from those at Tegea and, furthermore, have assigned the architect of the temple at Tegea, Skopas, to the Temple at Nemea as well. Although the buildings share several features (some of which are shared in general by 4th-century temples), they differ significantly in overall plan and design. While a conscious effort at Nemea to adopt some of the forms used at Tegea is likely, it does not follow that the same architect designed the two temples. It seems more rea-

88. *IG* II² 1668.55–59.

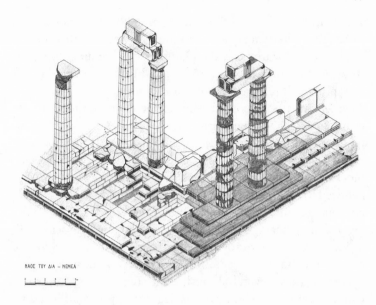

ΝΑΟΣ ΤΟΥ ΔΙΑ – ΝΕΜΕΑ

Fig. 54. Perspective drawing of the columns to be reconstructed in the first phase of the Temple reconstruction project.

sonable to suppose that there were artisans who worked on both projects, quite likely repeating some techniques and styles.[89]

Reconstruction Project. A detailed study of all the surviving architectural elements scattered around the Temple (Fig. 5) was begun in 1980 with the objective of eventually reconstructing the building.[90] Fallen blocks were moved and recorded individually (measured, drawn, and photographed)

89. See Hill, *op. cit.* (n. 80) 44, n. 107 for a summary of scholars who have argued that the same architect designed, or the same artisans constructed, the two temples. More telling evidence would seem to be the virtually identical method used for securing rafter to cornice block (see p. 144 and n. 86); structural details shared by the two buildings may have greater significance than stylistic details, which are more bound by convention.

90. See F. A. Cooper et al., *The Temple of Zeus at Nemea: Perspectives and Prospects* (Athens 1983) 51–83.

and then placed around the Temple in fields grouped by type to facilitate retrieval during rebuilding. Once the fallen material had been cleared and the platform and standing columns studied, the original position of each block was located and new plans and restored elevations drafted.

In March 1984 reconstruction of the third and fourth columns from the northeastern corner on the northern side of the Temple began (Fig. 54). Ancient blocks were removed, cleaned, repaired, and replaced, and some forty-two new blocks of the *krepidoma* were quarried from the same quarry believed to have been used by the Temple builders (see p. 134), cut, and set in place. For economic reasons work was suspended in January 1985 with seven more new blocks still needed before the restored stylobate would be ready to receive the columns. In addition to the newly set blocks, the visitor will see several alongside the Temple, including repaired column drums in various degrees of preparation waiting to be reset.

Sacred Square II

THE ALTAR OF ZEUS

About 10 m. east of the ramp of the Temple, a long low line of limestone blocks forms the foundation course of an altar. Sacrifice, the central part of ancient Greek worship, usually took place at an altar in front of a temple rather than inside it and was visible to all the worshipers standing around the altar. The unusually long Altar of Zeus (at least 41 m. when complete) runs along the entire facade of the Temple, with which it is aligned, and continues beyond the line of its northern side. The remains of another similarly long altar are preserved at the sanctuary of Poseidon at Isthmia.[91]

91. Broneer, *op. cit.* (n. 37) 98–101.

The end of the Altar is missing, as is shown by the *anathyrosis* on the northern end of the northernmost block, indicating that another stone was once set next to it. We will never know its actual length. Farmers in the Early Christian period probably ripped out the missing end; the remains of the Altar were never very deeply covered, and the last few stones at the north were gouged by recent plowing.

The triglyph altar in the museum courtyard (A 71; p. 72) was found about 35 m. northeast of this end of the Altar, and the base on which it has been placed (A 70 a, b), which probably supported it in antiquity, was uncovered about 7 m. northeast of the end of the long altar. The sanctuary probably extended in this direction where this altar, and doubtless other dedications still unexcavated, stood in an open area.

Near the northern end of the Altar, east of the last four hard limestone blocks, are the remains of softer stones, with channels cut in their tops. These seem to be reused blocks, perhaps from a water channel, here employed as curbing for the Altar, like the narrow rectangular blocks east and west of the Altar further south.

The part of the Altar north of the ramp of the Temple (Fig. 55) was composed of close-set horizontal courses of hard limestone rectangular blocks. Fragments of small votive vessels (like the ones on the top shelf, left, in case 5 in the museum; p. 30) found between stones near the northern end of the Altar show that this part was in use in the Archaic period. Pry marks for levering stones of a higher course into place can be seen on the tops of many of the preserved blocks. Two sets are visible on the stones in the row beside the curbing on the western side of the Altar, one set on the eastern side, another on the western. These may indicate two phases in the history of this part of the Altar.

The construction of the Altar is not uniform throughout its extant length, and it is easy to see that additions were made in antiquity. Although we cannot assign dates to them, their

Fig. 55. The northern end of the Altar of Zeus from the north.

positions relative to each other allow us to work out a chronology of sorts. A square block along the western side of the Altar and two rectangular blocks along with part of a third north of it make up part of a late (but undatable) addition; they were added after the row of curbing blocks just west of the Altar proper was set in place (which also probably occurred well after the northern part of the Altar had been constructed; see further p. 152). Further south two single blocks and one pair of blocks were also added after the main construction was complete. Some may be supports for a four-piered construction (a *tetrastylon* or *baldacchino*) over part of the Altar;[92] if this is the case, farmers have ripped out the corresponding bases on the eastern side.

92. Compare an altar at Perachora: H. Plommer and F. Salviat, "The Altar of Hera Akraia at Perachora," *BSA* 61 (1966) 207–15; for a general discussion of *tetrastyla,* see D. W. Rupp, *Greek Altars of the Northeastern Peloponnese c. 750/725 B.C. to c. 300/275 B.C.* (Ph.D. diss., Bryn Mawr College 1974) 359–75.

Fig. 56. The southern end of the Altar of Zeus from the south, with the double statue base in the foreground.

Opposite the ramp of the Temple is a gap in the stones of the Altar. This destruction, like that on the northern end, is the work of the Early Christian farmers, who pulled out some blocks to plant their crops in furrows adjacent to other blocks which survive today.

The construction technique for the southern part of the Altar differs from that for the northern part (Fig. 56); a core, mostly of softer material, is surrounded by harder rectangular stones. Traces of the core can be seen in the earth east of the western row of hard limestone blocks. Two blocks of hard stone are in place in the core, one at the edge of the gap at the

center of the Altar and another at the southeastern corner of
the Altar. Although the northern and southern parts were
constructed at different times, we can be fairly certain that at
some point they formed a coherent whole rather than two
separate altars side by side. One indication of this is the
curbstones which remain on the eastern and western sides of
the southern part of the Altar and on the western side of the
northern part. Setting lines on both rows of hard limestone
blocks in the southern part show where stones of a higher
course were aligned; traces of a corresponding line north of
the gap are further evidence of similar construction, at some
time, for both parts of the Altar. The original southern end
consisted of two L-shaped stones; at a later date an extension
was added to the south.

The long Altar, then, which was surely part of the 4th-
century sanctuary, includes an original northern section, in
existence during the lifetime of the Early Temple, and a southern addition. Curbing and the southern extension were added
later, though it is not clear when; these elements could have
been laid in place as soon as the southern part of the Altar had
been built. Blocks west of (and resting on) the western curbing were added last. The Altar as a whole had a long history.
A coin of Trajan (c 157; museum case 3) found just west of
the Altar near the gap shows that activity of some sort took
place here in the 2nd century after Christ.

Volutes frequently decorated the ends of other altars, various moldings were common, and a superstructure with triglyphs and metopes was used in this part of Greece. Lack of
evidence for such elements at Nemea does not prove that the
Altar was plain, but until such evidence is found we might
imagine a plain superstructure, set back about a third of a
meter from the outside edges of the preserved stones and supporting a long narrow tablelike top.

Although we know that sacrifices typically involved preliminary libations, prayers, cutting the animal's throat, divi-

Fig. 57. The southeastern corner of the Temple from the north-west, with associated monuments and planting pits for the Sacred Grove.

sion of the carcass, and, ultimately, feasting, we cannot be sure exactly what occurred here in front of the Temple of Zeus. A mixture of dark earth and tiny bits of burnt bone lying in bands beside the Altar shows that spilled debris was regularly swept up. We cannot know whether the length of the Altar meant that large numbers of animals were sacrificed simultaneously (in which case the noise, smell, smoke, and swarms of flies[93] must have been considerable) or that different parts of the Altar were reserved for different rituals (with a *tetrastylon* possibly over the part for the hero Opheltes).

93. Flies were a constant problem at ancient festivals, and at Olympia, for example, sacrifices at an altar of Zeus Apomyios (Averter of Flies) were said to drive the flies to the other side of the Alpheios River. See Pausanias 5.14.1 and the extensive commentary *ad loc.* by J. G. Frazer, *Pausanias's Description of Greece* III (London 1898) 558–59.

At the southern end of the Altar is a base for two statues. Traces of gouges made when two rectangular plinths were ripped out may be seen on the tops of the seven stones of the upper course. This course is not aligned with the stones below, probably because those stones belonged to an earlier base, which for some unknown reason was no longer in use when the upper course was set over it. Stones of the lower course carry traces of *anathyrosis;* they may be reused, or these surviving stones may be part of a larger construction, the rest of which was demolished before the higher course was added. The higher course and its two statues appear to have been erected around 330 B.C., during the same building program that produced the present Temple of Zeus.

The remains of two structures lie at the southeastern corner of the Temple (Fig. 57). Near the southern side several limestone blocks form part of a circle resting on a nearly square base. Up against these stones, just to the south, are the remains of a T-shaped structure, the Nu Structure (see p. 155), its two arms pointing north and south. From the southeastern foundation stones of the Temple there is a good view of these structures in relation to each other.

Several rectangular blocks of different sizes lie between the circular structure and the Temple itself. The steps of temples in Greek sanctuaries were often cluttered (to our minds) with official inscriptions in stone and dedications—the steps of the Parthenon on the Athenian Acropolis, for instance, had cuttings for inscribed stones.[94] We see here at Nemea separate bases for similar official or pious displays.

CIRCULAR STRUCTURE B

About three-quarters of a circle of hard limestone blocks is preserved around a core of decayed and "melted" softer stone.

---

94. G. P. Stevens, "The Setting of the Periclean Parthenon," *Hesperia,* suppl. 3 (1940), especially frontispiece and Figs. 20 and 66, and "The Northeast Corner of the Parthenon," *Hesperia* 15 (1946) 1–26, esp. Fig. 1.

Faint marks on the tops of some of the harder blocks show that a second, higher, course of stones was set back about 0.30 m. from the outer edge of the preserved course. Several blocks from higher courses of this monument were found during excavation, scattered elsewhere on the site. They enable a reconstruction on paper of a three-stepped base, perhaps for an altar or a statue. The highest course of the base is estimated to have been 3.54 m. in diameter. It appears to have supported another circular element approximately 1.60 m. in diameter.[95] Numerous bits of bronze were found in the earth around this base, so we know that a bronze statue or some other dedication stood nearby, perhaps on a base whose remains are preserved here. Although no part of a circular monument need have been emphasized, special attention seems to have been paid to the eastern quadrant of this structure. An irregularly shaped trench was dug in antiquity for the removal of stones at the east side of the monument. Its outline may indicate the presence at one time of some sort of projection or a small base for a dedication.

Circular Structure B seems to have been built in the second quarter of the 5th century B.C. It was apparently destroyed at the end of that century.

NU STRUCTURE

Hard against Circular Structure B and covering a small fraction of its surface is a T-shaped structure designated the Nu Structure, after a now-hidden mason's mark in the form of the Greek letter *nu* on one of its blocks. A facing of hard limestone blocks and a surrounding mass of softer stone, now decaying, once supported a higher course set back about 0.10 m. from the outside edge of the exterior stones. Apparently the layout of the Nu Structure differed slightly in an earlier phase; blocks which originally cut into the Circular Structure

95. See F. Salviat, "Le monument de Théogénès sur l'agora de Thasos," *BCH* 80 (1956) 147–60, for a monument similar to Circular Structure B.

have been removed from the northern wing, and a setting line near the northern edge of the block that is oriented approximately east–west in the northern wing indicates the placement of the next higher course of stones in the later phase.

No evidence dates either phase securely, nor can we be sure of the function of the Nu Structure. It overlays and is thus obviously later than the Circular Structure, which had long been destroyed when the Nu Structure was erected. The 4th-century surfacing of the area south of the Temple was laid down after the Nu Structure was in place; probably this monument is another of the constructions of the late 4th century. Its massive foundations indicate that it supported some considerable weight, and several marble blocks that belonged to the Nu Structure have been recognized as reused in the *bema* of the Early Christian Basilica. Some of these blocks belong to missing lower courses of the monument, but others, which belong to the highest course of the Nu Structure, have cuttings in their upper surfaces for the feet of statues, including an equestrian group, as mentioned earlier (p. 85). Fragments of bronze, including bits of statuary, were found in the earth around and over the remains of the Nu Structure, which must, then, have supported a large statue group.[96]

South of the Nu Structure is a rectangular base for another monument, probably also a statue.

The Sacred Square between the Temple and the Altar to the north and the *oikoi* to the south is a hard-packed surface, now patchy and broken through in places, which was laid down in the 4th century B.C. as part of the general refurbishment of the sanctuary. It replaced earlier surfaces that likely belonged to the Archaic sanctuary. No paths seem to have been deliberately laid out within this open space. The scatter of small

96. See O. Broneer, *Isthmia* II, *Topography and Architecture* (Princeton 1973) 12, for a rectangular monument with two wings of unequal size comparable to the Nu Structure.

finds and coins in a line running northwest–southeast on
the ancient surface in front of Oikos 9 suggests that people
walked diagonally across this part of the sanctuary, perhaps to
and from the Stadium. Dedications were doubtless erected in
the Sacred Square during the renewal of the sanctuary in the
late 4th century B.C. as well as in the Archaic and Classical
periods. A base from one such dedication of the earlier phase
of the sanctuary can be seen in the courtyard of the museum
(I 8, to Artemis Ephodia or Hekate Ephodia; see p. 72).

SACRED GROVE

A grove of about two dozen cypress trees has recently been
planted where trees stood in antiquity. Circular patches of
soft dark earth found during the excavation of this part of the
Sacred Square proved to be the filling for clearly definable
hemispherical pits (Fig. 58). Small veins of dark earth extended beyond the bottoms and sides of several pits, and
some pits contained stones that might have anchored seed-
lings during planting. The identification of these pits as remnants of a Sacred Grove is supported by references in ancient
literature to trees around the Temple of Zeus. Analysis of soil
from the pits suggests that they contained cypresses (trees
which, in fact, the traveler Pausanias tells us grew around the
Temple). The layout of the restored grove is that of the late
4th century B.C. No doubt trees were replaced after that time
when necessary. Euripides, Pindar, and perhaps Simonides
mention a sacred grove, and therefore the 4th-century planting was not the first at Nemea.[97]

Sacred groves in ancient Greece were common at rural,
suburban, and urban sanctuaries, whether these were simple

97. Euripides, *Hercules Furens* 359–60; *Hypsipyle,* fr. Iiv.10 and frr. 22 +
60ii.108 (ed. Bond); Pindar, *Nemean* 2.4–5; and perhaps Simonides, fr. 22 (ed.
Diehl = fr. 507 ed. Page).

Fig. 58. The planting pits for the Sacred Grove, from the southeast.

open-air shrines or elaborate building complexes. But although ancient Greek literature of all genres and periods makes many passing references to them, practically no physical evidence survives. The visitor to Athens, however, can see another example around the Hephaisteion, where shrubs have been planted in ancient rock-cut pits.[98] For examples closer to Nemea, we have written testimony to sacred groves on the citadels of Phlious and Acrocorinth, in the Asklepieion at Epidauros, and near the city of Argos.[99] We know of no ritual that was performed exclusively in a sacred grove. On a

98. D. B. Thompson, "The Garden of Hephaistos," *Hesperia* 6 (1937) 396–425.

99. Phlious: Pausanias 2.13.3–4. Acrocorinth: Pindar, fr. 107 (ed. Bowra) *apud* Athenaeus, 13.573f–574a. Epidauros: Aeschines, *Anth. Gr.* 6.330; *IG* IV² 121.90–94, 120–21; *IG* IV² 123.1–3; *IG* IV² 618; Pausanias 2.27.1–7. Near Argos: Herodotus 6.78–80; Pausanias 2.20.8 and 3.4.1.

practical level, groves of trees provided shade for visitors, and in historical and legendary times they were places of religious and political asylum. Long-lived, they seem to have been considered living connections with events of the legendary past.[100]

BOUNDARY STONES

Among the trees lie the stubs of three stones, about 0.30 m. on each side, about 12 m. apart, roughly 20 m. north of the facades of the *oikoi*. The easternmost stone is now surrounded by a pile of loose stones at the edge of the excavated area.

The size, shape, and location (see Fig. 10) of these three stones indicate that they served as *horoi*, "boundary markers," perhaps marking off a special area of intense sanctity near the Temple from a subsidiary part of the sanctuary where the *oikoi* were situated. During excavation the 4th-century surface of the Sacred Square was found to continue up to the sides of the stones, indicating that they had been set in place before the surface was laid. If so, the stones may have had nothing to do with the Sacred Grove of the 4th-century refurbishment of the sanctuary. They may have marked a smaller sacred area, connected with the Early Temple, which did not cover as much territory as the Sacred Grove did later. Their stubs would have been left in place although they no longer marked a boundary that was observed in the 4th-century sanctuary.

One assumes that the tops of these uninscribed and unimpressive stones have been broken off; if their missing upper parts bore inscriptions, they may have been similar to the one on the stone I 107 now in the museum (see p. 33), found just

---

100. For Greek sacred groves in general, see D. Birge, *Sacred Groves in the Ancient Greek World* (Ph.D. diss., University of California, Berkeley, 1982).

northeast of the northeastern corner of Oikos 9. Its inscription, which may be translated literally as "Boundary of the Flat Area," presumably referring to the open space of the sanctuary defined on the south, for example, by the facades of the *oikoi*, may give us the official name of the Sacred Square, Epipola. Although of comparable size, this stone cannot be joined with any of the boundary stones still on the site. Given its date of the late 4th century B.C. (based on the style of its letters), it is likely to come from the reconstruction and renewal project in the Sanctuary of Zeus.

The Oikoi II

At the southeastern corner of the Sacred Square lie the final three *oikoi* in the series.

OIKOS 7

In Oikos 7 evidence of the widespread disturbance of this area by Early Christian irrigation ditches and farming plots is visible: large trenches cut perpendicularly through most of its east wall and eastern half. The west wall is preserved in places above the poros foundations, showing some of the rubble socle which would, in turn, have supported mud-brick walls. Some remnants of mud brick were found in this *oikos*. The three interior bases, 0.70 m. square and uniformly 5.20 m. apart on centers, are visible along the north-south axis. A small fragment of a Doric capital (A 88) found within the building along with another, similar, fragment found south of it (A 86) may have been associated with these roof supports. A series of hard gray limestone blocks of various sizes, reused here in a line from the southern interior base to the eastern side wall, is a later effort to divide the large single room into smaller rooms. The poorly preserved limestone block west of the southern base in the same line is probably also part of this later partition wall, to judge from the material, construction technique, and relative elevations. A series of Lakonian roof tiles, including two stamped fragments (AT 27 and 28) and a fragment of an *opaion* tile (AT 29), were also found along the east wall of this *oikos* and can probably be associated with the building.

The *opaion* tile may be more easily associated with Oikos 8, however, where there was a greater need for this sort of tile pierced with a hole for ventilation.

OIKOS 8

Oikos 8, nearly square, measures 11.55 by 11.95 m. The single row of poros stones of its northern foundations has been robbed out, but a central hard limestone support base remains, as does a quantity of the rubble socle which once supported mud-brick walls. The east wall of the *oikos* continues past the south wall for 6.30 m. and then doglegs west 2.35 m. and south again 5.90 m. At that point it joins an east-west wall coming from the east wall of Oikos 9 to join the so-called Dining Establishment further west. This east-west wall is contemporary with Oikos 8, Oikos 9, the Dining Establishment, and the continuation of the east wall of Oikos 9. Like the other *oikoi,* these elements were all built in the first half of the 5th century B.C. Since these contemporary walls connect the three buildings and the areas between them, they must have functioned in part as a unit. A doorway in the south wall of Oikos 8 near the east wall once connected the *oikos* with the walled-in area to the south. This doorway was subsequently closed off by two large reused limestone blocks. The area behind Oikos 8 also communicated with that behind Oikos 9 through a doorway 0.95 m. wide, visible as a gap in the foundations of the eastern extension wall of Oikos 8 in the section south of its western jog.

A roof-support base just west of that western jog and another base approximately 3.20 m. due north indicate that part of the area behind Oikos 8 was roofed over at one time. A plastered and finished unfluted Doric column capital (A 124) found near the doorway between this area and that behind Oikos 9 may be associated with one of these two support bases. The northern base is slightly higher than the other, but this may indicate only that it was a later additional support. A few flat stones preserved in the corner formed by the eastern extension wall of Oikos 8 and the western jog of that same wall may have been paving stones for this back room.

During the third quarter of the 5th century B.C. Oikos 8 and its back room were taken over by a bronze sculpting workshop. The *oikos* was also remodeled, either at this time or later, and, like many of the other *oikoi,* was probably damaged in the 5th-century B.C. destruction of the sanctuary. The renovations cannot be dated precisely, but ceramic evidence places them after 450 B.C. The remodeling of the *oikos* included the closing of the doorway between it and the back room and the addition of a light, foundationless wall connecting the northernmost base of the back room with the south wall of the *oikos.* Some of this wall was preserved when excavated just northwest of that northern base. An external stairway, also added along the eastern side of the *oikos,* is visible only as a series of stones just north of the *oikos's* south wall. This staircase seems to have led to a room above the back room of the *oikos.*

The bronze sculptor's workshop extended throughout the southeastern section of the *oikos* and its back room, and even into the western section of Oikos 9. This workshop is attested by a large number of casting pits cut into the floors of these *oikoi.* These pits and the area surrounding them were discovered filled with ash, carbon, bronze drippings, and a variety of tools, the more significant of which are on display in case 20 in the museum (see pp. 63–64 for the technique of bronze casting employed in this shop).

Fig. 59. "Smelting" furnace in Oikos 8, from the west.

A large circular pit just east of the center of Oikos 8 and a neighboring rectangular pit to the south were two of the most productive of these casting pits. From them came a large mortar, fragments of a 5th-century red-figure kylix, and a quantity of casting armature. Directly east, another large casting pit lies flush against the *oikos* wall. The molds (TC 59) and the large stone basin (ST 362) shown *in situ* in a photograph displayed in the museum also came from this pit. This basin, placed upside down in the pit, shows signs of wear on its bottom surface, indicating that it served here as a sort of paving stone.

In the back room of Oikos 8 the bronze caster's furnace stands just northeast of the northern base (Fig. 59). This furnace consists of a circular pit 0.95 m. in diameter and 0.50 m. deep. The southern portion of the pit had a clay roof with four holes over which bronze was melted for pouring into the

molds. A 4th-century B.C. well, just northwest of the northern base, was also excavated in this back room to its full depth
of 4.91 m. Probably it was never completed or was used for
only a short time when the water table was high. Although
this well may have been associated with the bronze-casting
activity, it could also relate to another suggested use of the
back room, as a cooking or kitchen area.

OIKOS 9

Like Oikos 8, Oikos 9 is a simple rectangle, 11.20 by 14.50
m. with one central hard limestone support base. Although
constructed at the same time as Oikos 8, Oikos 9 had a much
shorter history, only a few decades, and had already been
damaged by the time of the bronze-casting activity in the
third quarter of the 5th century B.C. This sequence is attested
by the two bronze-casting pits that cut into the west wall of
the *oikos*. In the northern pit a foundation block of the west
wall had been worked down to form a sort of ledge or shelf
for the bronze-casting operations.

There is also ceramic evidence that the double row of
poros foundations of the north wall of the *oikos* had already
been robbed out by the late 5th century B.C. This robbing
trench contained many of the architectural elements of the facade of the *oikos*, including A 128–135, on display in the museum courtyard. By putting these elements together with the
architectural elements subsequently found rebuilt into the annex of Oikos 9, it was possible to make an accurate reconstruction of the facade of Oikos 9 (Fig. 60; see pp. 67–70).
Since all these elements were found in a context clearly associated with the *oikos*, the reconstruction is secure, including the
association of the Doric *anta* capital (A 133) with the other
Ionic elements. Although stylistically the molding profiles of
these elements suggest slightly different dates, generally these
dates overlap and span the period of the building's occupation. The profile of one Ionic base clearly associated with the

Fig. 60. The reconstructed facade of Oikos 9.

building, however, has previously been classified as first appearing on the Temple of Apollo at Bassae in about 420 B.C., a date later than the destruction of Oikos 9.[101]

Although the main portion of Oikos 9 was short-lived, like Oikos 8 it has a back room, walled in by a zigzagging continuation of its east wall, which remained in use after the *oikos* proper had been destroyed. That this back room was built at the same time as the *oikos* can be demonstrated by the block of the east wall of the *oikos* abutting the south wall, extending partly into the *oikos* and partly into the back room, bonding the two walls. Clearly the back room was already planned when this block of the *oikos* was set in place. This east wall continues past the south wall for 4.60 m., then turns due west 2.65 m. and south again 4.10 m. to meet the east-west wall which ultimately connects with the Dining Establishment. That this back area was also roofed over at one time is shown by a hard limestone base centrally located west of the western jog in the continuation wall.

Several stone slabs can be seen just north of the corner formed where the east wall jogs west. These slabs, originally

101. L. T. Shoe, *The Profiles of Greek Mouldings* (Cambridge, Mass. 1936) 180 and Pls. LVIII, LXVI, and LXIII.

thought to be paving stones, seem to form a bench. Below the southwestern corner of it were discovered a volcanic stone slab and grinder used in the preparation of flour. Directly west lies a rectangular clay-lined pit, found filled with carbon, ash, and bone, which appears to have been a roasting pit. The slabs, stones, and pit are all later additions, and they seem to indicate that this was once a cooking area.

Two unlined wells southwest and southeast of the column base of this back-room area may also support the idea that this was once a cooking area. The western well, 6.80 m. deep, was closed in the late 4th century B.C. Probably quite short-lived, like the well in the back room of Oikos 8, it may have been in use during only one festival, if it was ever completed. The eastern well, from the second quarter of the 5th century B.C., attained a depth of only 0.93 m., suggesting that it was never completed.

The use of the back room of Oikos 9 as a cooking area, as well as the possible use of the back rooms of Oikoi 8 and 1 for the same purpose, is unprecedented in connection with other treasuries and *oikoi*. Evidence of food preparation in conjunction with these *oikoi* can be explained only if the connected rectangular building to the southwest is identified as a dining establishment. At the time when these buildings all communicated with each other, the back rooms seem to have functioned as kitchens to supply the Dining Establishment and perhaps other *oikoi*. We will return to this topic when we visit the Dining Establishment.

When the area east of Oikos 9 was cleared in 1983, the remains of an "annex" to it were discovered. These remains, from the Hellenistic period, consist of a rubble foundation with larger blocks on top, many of them reused architectural elements, including several from the long-since-destroyed Oikos 9. Many of these elements have been removed from the annex, including the corner capital from Oikos 9 (A 244; see Fig. 21), two segments of engaged columns (A 240 and

241), two large Doric column drums (A 246 and 247), and a faceted column drum (A 245) similar to that on display in the museum courtyard (A 30; see p. 73).

DINING ESTABLISHMENT

The Dining Establishment, located immediately south of Oikos 7, is attached to Oikoi 8 and 9 by the east-west wall which forms their back rooms. The rectangular building has external dimensions of 9.82 by 7.44 m. A north-south wall divides it into two chambers: the western room measures 1.90 by 6.10 m. on the interior; the eastern room measures 6.65 by 6.10 m. The off-center doorway in the west wall of each room suggests the use of the building as a dining establishment: offsetting the doors allows the maximum number of rectangular dining couches to be fitted around the periphery of a room. If the average size of such dining couches was 0.85 by 1.80 m., eleven couches could have fit neatly around the perimeter of the eastern room.[102] Evidence that food was prepared and consumed aids in this identification. Furthermore, only 6.20 m. west of the entrance of the Dining Establishment a rectangular pit, 1.35 by 0.70 m. and approximately 1.00 m. deep, was found lined with small stones and sealed, apparently intentionally, with an informal vault of similar stones. The fine ware (mostly drinking vessels) in the pit dates from the second quarter of the 5th century B.C. Intermixed with it was a large amount of ash and pig bones, including one jaw of a wild boar. This pit, apparently of a sacrificial nature, may have held the remains of ritual dining.

A well immediately northwest of the Dining Establishment probably supplied water for the building.

102. For the underlying principles involved in restoring couches around the perimeter of ancient dining rooms, see S. G. Miller, *The Prytaneion* (Berkeley 1978) 219–24.

Although no direct evidence dates this building, which is assumed to have been constructed contemporaneously with Oikoi 8 and 9, there is evidence that it must have been destroyed by the mid 3rd century B.C. By that time both it and the kilns in the area had been leveled and covered over by a layer of gravel to serve as a *plateia,* or open square, next to the Xenon.

THE KILNS

Although covered over by earth as of this writing, the region just in front and southwest of the Dining Establishment produced the complex of four kilns used to manufacture roof tiles for the building program in the last third of the 4th century B.C. (see Fig. 20 and Temple of Zeus, p. 168). It is hoped that it will soon be possible to erect a shelter to display the workings of this interesting monument. For the moment, we must be content with the description already given on pages 64–66.

The Xenon II: Eastern End and Aqueduct

The remains of the Xenon southeast of the Dining Establishment are completely exposed, unobscured by the Basilica (whose apse is visible to the west). The most striking feature of the eastern end of the Xenon is the drastic difference in masonry between Rooms 15 and 16 and the rest of the building. All the walls except the west wall of Rooms 15 and 16 are constructed of rough, uncut field stones fitted together haphazardly and insecurely. By contrast, the west wall has a broad foundation of cut poros blocks surmounted by rectangularly cut orthostates about 0.80 m. tall. This wall, in fact, was an exterior wall until Rooms 15 and 16, whose walls strikingly resemble those of the annex of Oikos 9, were hastily tacked onto the original building (see p. 166).

Two columnar objects, the base of a *perirrhanterion* in Room 14 and an altar in Room 13 to the south, belong either to this remodeling or, more likely, to the second, late 3rd-century, use of the building. Both objects imply a religious use for at least these two rooms in the second phase, but the exact use is unclear.

Before moving south into Room 13, we can note two of the three column foundations in Room 14, the third one on the plan (see Fig. 30) having been restored for symmetry. An octagonal column and capital in the museum courtyard (A 30 and 181) and other matching octagonal columns (including several reused in a late wall in Room 8) have long been associated with these foundations. In light of the restoration (Fig. 31), however, this association seems less likely. One column drum was found in Room 13, pressed into the floor and above a roof tile. Its situation suggests that the octagonal columns and capitals belonged to the second story from which this drum fell during the destruction of the original Xenon.

In the south wall of Room 14, the median wall of the Xenon, there are several reused blocks, including Ionic half columns from the facade of Oikos 9 (see pp. 67–70 and 164).

Room 13 has the best-preserved walls in the whole Xenon. The second large block from the south in the west wall has the inscription ΕΠΙΔΑΥΡΙΩΝ (I 31; see pp. 71 and 119). On the inside surface of the spur walls which project into the room from the south wall, drafted margins are cut along the edges. These margins, which occur on miscellaneous blocks elsewhere (for example in the south wall of Room 8), are part of the evidence that the Xenon is a recycled building, constructed of blocks from other buildings. Cuttings for a double-leaved door can be seen in the threshold blocks of Room 13. Above this threshold the starting block (A 100) was discovered, reused; it can be seen in the museum (see p. 35).

This block also gives evidence for a remodeling phase in the Xenon, one which perhaps took place at the time Rooms 15 and 16 were added to the eastern end.

In front of the south door of Room 13, a stretch of the aqueduct is visible. Several of its cover tiles here differ from those nearer the Bath; they are Lakonian, from the ridge of a roof—probably the original Xenon roof—and were used to make repairs to the water channel. Beyond the threshold of the door is a stone cover slab, placed over the aqueduct to protect it. A similar slab covers the aqueduct at the threshold of Room 11 as well; at the doorway of Room 3 an extra layer of tiles was used. These stone slabs and tiles suggest that the Xenon was built shortly before the aqueduct in the late 4th century B.C.

V

THE STADIUM

As of this writing, the Stadium is not normally open, and visitors must petition the guards to accompany them. The easiest approach to the Stadium is made by retracing the route of the museum access road south to the main asphalt road and turning left (east) onto it. After two turns of the road, the first left and the second right at a modern wayside shrine, there is a gate. The road that bisected the ancient Stadium (Fig. 61) was cut and excavation beneath it begun in May 1989.

Visitors, after leaving the modern asphalt road and proceeding to the crest of the ridge west of the Stadium track, may wish to pause at the bench for a good general view of the Nemean Stadium, which was excavated from 1974 to 1981. The Stadium was created by taking advantage of a natural amphitheater between two ridges which extended north from Evangelistria Hill. The earth removed in hollowing out a semicircle at the southern end was dumped at the northern end, creating an artificial terrace approximately 8.25 m. high for the northernmost third of the racetrack. The track originally extended 600 ancient feet, a measurement standard in Greek stadia.[103] A retaining wall, however, was not built to

---

103. The ancient Greek word σтάδιον meant, originally, a unit of length (600 feet), then the name of a race of that distance (see p. 4), and finally the place where the race of that length took place. The word *stadium* retains only part of

enclose the fill of the terrace.[104] The northern end of the Stadium consequently eroded long ago, and the northern end of the ancient track is missing.

The major elements of the Stadium, including the vaulted entranceway on the western side of the track and the water channel around its periphery, date from the late 4th century B.C. (see pp. 185–86).

From the bench the eastern side of the track to the north is visible, including the water channel—a characteristic feature of ancient stadia—constructed of fairly hard poros limestone, which supplied athletes and spectators with fresh drinking water.[105] One of the stone settling basins placed at intervals along the water channel is also visible, as well as a stone pillar which marks the 400-foot point from the starting line.

The Track

At the bottom of the slope on the western side of the racetrack a row of reused stone blocks was discovered less than 1.00 m. west of the stone water channel and essentially parallel to it. Some of these blocks retain traces of "ice-tong" lifting holes.[106] This row of blocks, approximately 0.08–0.10 m. lower than the water channel, was a sidewalk. Stratigraphic and numismatic evidence indicates that both the sidewalk and the stone water channel were constructed in the late 4th century B.C.[107] The lower area between the sidewalk and water channel functioned as a storm drain to carry off rainwater.

---

the last meaning. See pages 176–77 on foot lengths at Nemea and other Greek stadia.

104. See *Hesperia* 51 (1982) 36–37.

105. For the stadium at Epidauros: P. Kavvadias, Πρακτικά (1902) Pls. A′ and B′; and R. Patrucco, *Lo Stadio di Epidauro* (Florence 1976) Figs. 14, IV.2, XI.1, XIII.2. For the stadium at Olympia: Mallwitz, *op. cit.* (n. 62) 181–84.

106. See p. 60 for the original use of such blocks in the Early Temple of Zeus.

107. See *Hesperia* 46 (1977) 26, and *Hesperia* 49 (1980) 202–3.

Fig. 61. Aerial view of the Stadium, 1980: A = Judges' stand; B = "Water closet"; C = West end of tunnel.

Immediately north of the path of the visitor who descends to the racetrack is a stone settling basin in the line of the water channel. Although no ancient source explicitly indicates the purpose of such basins, it seems reasonable to believe that in them dirt and debris settled out of the water flowing along the channel. They may also have provided drinking water for athletes and spectators. Several settling basins in the Stadium preserve traces of the red hydraulic cement with which they were originally coated, as do many of the blocks of the water channel itself.

A meter or so north of the settling basin is a 0.27 m. square stone pillar, broken across the top, marking the 300-foot point from the starting line.

The track surface itself is hard-packed gray-green clay, but it has been covered over with sand in recent times to protect it from the weather. To prepare the track for the Nemean Games and to maintain its level below that of the water channel, the track surface was dug up, leveled, and rolled every two years. This practice is attested at other sites, including the Stadium at Delphi.[108] Thus the track surface was maintained at the same height from the time of the Stadium's construction in the late 4th century B.C. until the second half of the 4th century after Christ, the latter date based on ceramic and numismatic evidence.[109]

On the eastern side of the track are the water channel, water basin, and 300-foot marker, all of which correspond to those on the western side of the track, although the marker on the western side is better preserved than its counterpart. East of and parallel to the water channel are a few scattered limestone blocks, their purpose uncertain. They may have

108. For the 3rd-century B.C. inscription that records preparations for the Pythian Games, see J. Pouilloux, "Travaux à Delphes à l'occasion des Pythia," *BCH* suppl. 4 (1977) 106, lines 23–24. Pickaxes and, to a lesser extent, rollers are frequently depicted in athletic scenes in vase painting.

109. *Hesperia* 47 (1978) 84. That the track stayed at more or less the same level does not imply that it was being used for games. There is no evidence for games at Nemea after the 3rd century B.C.

served either as the foundation for a wooden judges' stand or as a short row of *proedria,* "front-row seats," for important visitors to the Nemean Games.

South along the eastern edge of the Stadium track is another settling basin as well as a stone pillar. The pillar, which has a counterpart on the western side of the track, marks the 200-foot point from the starting line and shows that originally these markers rose some 0.45 m. above the Stadium floor. The shallow hole on the top surface indicates that some further element was carried on the marker. Immediately east of the marker and parallel to the water channel a strip of reddish earth, now covered over, was found. This represents the decomposed remains of a terracotta water channel which turned a meter or so south of the 200-foot marker and cut through the stone water channel. The path of this terracotta channel also cut across the racecourse to the west and through the surface of the track and then was routed into the vaulted entrance tunnel, passing through a "homemade" settling basin (see p. 36). These features clearly indicate that it was constructed when the track and the stone water channel were no longer being used for the Nemean Games. Although the precise date of these developments is uncertain,[110] evidence discovered in the entrance tunnel indicates that the water channel had been constructed by the mid 1st century after Christ at the latest (see p. 186 and n. 128). It provided water for some unknown purpose outside and west of the Stadium.

Further south along the eastern edge of the track is a row of squared stone blocks that begins approximately 25 m. from the 200-foot marker and is set against the stone water channel. Ceramic evidence indicates that these blocks, as well as the contemporary water channel, date from the second half of the 4th century B.C.[111] Immediately east of the water channel, parallel both to it and to the row of stone blocks, the re-

110. *Hesperia* 49 (1980) 200–201.
111. *Hesperia* 46 (1977) 25.

Fig. 62. Judges' stand, basin, and socket for 100-foot marker, from the east.

mains of a mud-brick wall, now covered with earth, were discovered along with several iron and bronze nails and pins; the mud-brick and stone blocks probably supported a raised wooden platform that served as a judges' stand.[112]

Situated in the line of stone blocks is another stone settling basin. The block immediately north of it has a 0.28 by 0.12 m. rectangular cutting in its southeastern corner (Fig. 62). This cutting, which held the 100-foot marker, is 29.63 m. from the starting line, which gives a foot length of over 0.296 m. for the Nemean Stadium and a total length of approximately 178 m. for the 600-foot track. A similar foot length was used in the stadium at Delphi,[113] and it is original to the

112. Although the judges' stand in the stadium at Olympia is somewhat further down the track from the starting line, its general position is analogous to that suggested here at Nemea; cf. Mallwitz, *op. cit.* (n. 62) 181–82.

113. P. Aupert, *Fouilles de Delphes,* II, *Topographie et architecture: Le Stade* (Paris 1979) 43. Cf. C. M. Robinson and J. W. Graham, *Olynthus,* VIII, *The Hellenic House* (Baltimore 1938) 47–51; and A. W. Parsons in *Corinth,* III.ii, *The Defenses of Acrocorinth and the Lower Town,* ed. R. Carpenter and A. Bonn (Cambridge, Mass. 1936) 291–92.

4th-century Stadium here at Nemea, to judge from stratigraphic evidence showing the 100-foot markers and the water
channels to be contemporary.[114] The markers, however, were
not set with absolute precision. For example, the distance between the 100-foot and 200-foot markers on the eastern side
of the track is 29.62 m. rather than 29.63 m., and the 200-foot
marker on the western side of the track is 29.67 m. from the
cutting for the 100-foot marker. In addition, the 300-foot
markers on the eastern and western sides of the track are, respectively, 29.78 and 29.71 m. from their corresponding 200-
foot markers. Finally, the eastern 400-foot marker is less than
29.75 m. from the corresponding 300-foot marker. Such irregularities in the placement of distance markers occur also at
Epidauros (the only other site from antiquity with 100-foot
markers), where the intervals are even less precise than here at
Nemea.[115]

The lack of precision in the placement of the markers reveals ancient attitudes toward athletics. The irregularities in
the Nemean foot length may suggest that the markers served
as visual aids for athletes, judges, and spectators rather than
as a means to establish the precise distance of runners from
the starting line. One might add that the variations in foot
length within and between Greek stadia would have made
time records virtually meaningless, even if precise time mea-
surements had been technically possible or desirable. Competition in antiquity was man-to-man, not man-to-machine.

The width of the track at Nemea is also irregular. The distance between the water channel on the eastern and western

114. *Hesperia* 49 (1980) 201–2.
115. On the north side of the track at Epidauros, the successive 100-foot intervals from the east to the west starting line are as follows: 30.40, 30.11, 30.21,
30.10, 30.21, 30.27 m. On the southern side of the track, the first three corresponding intervals (the 400- and 500-foot markers are not extant) are 30.47,
30.18, and 30.19 m. See Kavvadias, *op. cit.* (n. 105) 86 and Pl. A'.

sides of the track increases from 23.52 m. at the southern starting line to 25.58 m. at the 100-foot markers, 26.66 m. at the 200-foot markers, and 26.93 m. at the 300-foot markers.[116] It has been suggested that at other sites such a "bulge" in the track allowed the spectators a better view; they could more easily look past their neighbors.[117]

Besides its variation in width, the track has a surface which slopes downward almost 2 m. from its southern to northern end. This slope must have been considered unimportant in its effect on athletic competition, since each runner would encounter the same difficulty. It was necessary, however, to achieve an adequate flow of drinking water in the stone water channel.

The water channel continues past the starting line and the settling basin at its eastern end to the closed, southern, end of the Nemean Stadium, hollowed out of Evangelistria Hill, which visitors may ascend for an excellent view of the whole Stadium (the best approach is from above the tunnel, following the line of the fence and the cypress trees planted alongside it). The slopes of the amphitheater are lined with informal seats irregularly carved into the soft bedrock (now covered over and planted to prevent erosion). Along with a section of stone blocks which forms a *proedria* along the western side of the track, these seating ledges around the southern end of the Stadium are the only permanent seats known in the Nemean Stadium. Nevertheless, the Stadium is estimated to have held as many as forty thousand spectators.

Water was supplied by terracotta pipes, four of which were discovered *in situ* on the southeastern slopes of the closed end of the Stadium (see museum, p. 35). The line of these pipes

116. The smaller increase as one reaches the midpoint of the track at the 300-foot marker suggests that the track begins to narrow again toward its northern end.

117. E.g., at Delphi, see Aupert, *op. cit.* (n. 113) 178.

was broken, with only scattered fragments further to the east, so that only the general direction from which the water came is known. Although it cannot be proved the ultimate source of the Stadium's water, the only possible source now known does lie to the east—the spring that supplied the Bath (see pp. 110–11 and Fig. 38).

The pipes brought the water to the southern end of the Stadium where three stone slabs stand on end, on three sides of another settling basin. The southern slab is pierced by a hole through which the water flowed from the pipe to the basin. The fourth side of the basin rests against, but at right angles to, another basin, and water flowed through notches in the side walls from the first to the second. The second basin is equipped with notches on its eastern and western sides (i.e., perpendicular to the line of the water flow from pipe to first to second basin), and these notches allowed for the flow of water into the stone channel which traces a semicircle here at the closed end of the Stadium. Once in the channel, the water continued down either side of the track with interruptions at settling basins, the first pair of which is at either end of the starting line (see Fig. 63), the second at the judges' stand (see Fig. 62), and so forth.

A limestone base is also at each end of the starting line. The eastern base consists of two superimposed rectangular blocks, the lower one 0.16 m. longer and wider. The base at the western end of the starting line consists of a single block, carved as though it were two blocks set one atop the other (Fig. 63). The length and width of its upper and lower elements are in approximately the same proportion as the upper and lower blocks of the eastern base. The upper surface of each base has been provided with a recessed panel. Near the center of this panel on the eastern base is a shallow circular cutting; the western base has no cutting but does have an enigmatic horizontal hole cut diagonally through its southwestern corner.

Fig. 63. Western end of starting line in the Stadium, with stone base, water channel, settling basin, and sidewalk, from the south.

Although the purpose of the two bases is uncertain, they may have supported statues.[118] Two black marble bases from around 300 B.C., found near the starting line, may have supported statues of victors in the Nemean Games (see p. 37).

Even more uncertain is the purpose of a block 0.91 by 0.42 m. immediately north of the settling basin at the western end of the starting line. The placement of this block, however, involved a westward adjustment in the course of the water channel, as indicated by the double cutting for the exit of the northern channel of the settling basin.

The starting line itself is 21.15 m. long, measured between the eastern and western bases. It consists of stone slabs with two parallel grooves for the athletes' feet cut into their upper

118. Cf. the similar bases in the later stadium at Isthmia: Broneer, *op. cit.* (n. 96) 56–57, plan 6. Also compare the cuttings on the upper surface of a base for two statues south of the Altar of Zeus (see p. 154) for analogous recessed "panels."

Fig. 64. The ancient starting stance at the line.

surface. Although the southern face of each groove is nearly vertical, the northern face is cut at an oblique angle to the upper surface of the starting line. Such grooves are characteristic of starting lines in ancient stadia, including those at Olympia, Epidauros, and Delphi.[119] The grooves seem uncomfortably close to one another for the modern athlete accustomed to a four-point starting stance for foot races, but the ancient stance was erect, as seen in Figure 64 and documented in many ancient depictions.[120]

The northern groove is cut continuously across the length of the starting line. The southern groove, however, is interrupted at regular intervals by gaps of approximately 0.25 m.

119. Olympia: Mallwitz, *op. cit.* (n. 62) 184–85; Epidauros: Kavvadias, *op. cit.* (n. 105) Pls. A': A, A"; B': 1, 3, 6, 10, 10', and Patrucco, *op. cit.* (n. 105) Figs. 21, XXVII.1, XXVII.2, XXIX.3, XXX.1; Delphi: Aupert, *op. cit.* (n. 113) Figs. 124–26. Note the differences in the distances between the grooves at the various sites. Standardization seems to have existed, if at all, only at a given site.

120. E. Norman Gardiner, *Athletics of the Ancient World* (Oxford 1930) 135. Upright stances were practiced until Thomas Burke introduced the four-point stance at the 1896 Olympics, where his victory in the 100 m. did much to bring this stance into popularity.

In each gap a square socket was cut, approximately 0.08 m. on a side and an average of 1.63 m. from the next socket, to hold a vertical post. Twelve such posts divided the original starting line into thirteen lanes. Later the starting line was provided with an additional, more closely spaced, set of twelve cuttings. Presumably at the same time, the original cuttings were filled in. Almost all the later cuttings are approximately 1.30 m. apart. Unlike the original cuttings, these postholes are placed without regard to the southern groove of the starting line. Two of them, moreover, cut through the southern groove. Although these later cuttings measure approximately 0.10 m. on a side, the lead still preserved in three of them indicates that the projecting posts were 0.07 m. square.

Another major change in the starting line is indicated by the stone block that projects from the northern edge of the starting line near each of its ends. The projection near the eastern end has a wide central cutting on a north-south axis. On the bottom surface of this cutting a series of shallow cuttings run parallel to each other and at right angles to the starting line. In addition, the eastern side of the projection has another cutting that is perpendicular to and intercepts the wide central cutting. The projection near the western end of the starting line is similar to the eastern projection in the arrangement of its cuttings. It is constructed from a single reused block, however, and has an oblique cutting on its western, rather than its eastern, side.

Because the two projecting additions are cut into the blocks of the starting line between the first and second original square cuttings at each end, and because they respect the second set of posthole cuttings, they are evidently contemporary with the later modification in the size of the running lanes. The projecting blocks almost certainly supported the mechanism (*hysplex*) used to start the races, although the precise nature of that mechanism is uncertain. Similar projecting blocks exist in the stadium at Epidauros, the later stadium at Isthmia, and the racecourse in the Corinthian Forum.[121]

Out in the racetrack, 5.30 m. north of the starting line and 3.40 m. west of the center of the track, is a limestone block, 0.56 m. on a side, its upper surface level with the surface of the track. From a square hole in the upper surface a *kampter,* or vertical turning post, projected, probably of wood, marking the turning point at the south end of the Stadium. (Ancient races were run up and down the track, not around the track as today.) The base for a similar turning post presumably existed in a comparable position at the opposite end of the Stadium.

Further north along the western side of the track a row of stone blocks, immediately west of the water channel, marks the continuation of the sidewalk we first encountered upon entering the Stadium.

The row of stone blocks just west of the sidewalk, like the sidewalk itself, consists of reused material. The row extends, however, only to the Stadium entrance. Its blocks, 0.27 m. higher than the sidewalk, form the *proedria* previously mentioned. In some places, a third row of blocks is preserved, some of them actually cut from the bedrock *in situ,* which formed a second row of seats.

North of a settling basin, some 28.30 m. north of the starting line, two large limestone blocks are set against the eastern face of the water channel. The southern block preserves the remains of a 0.28 m. square cutting which held the 100-foot marker. These blocks, opposite the foundations for the judges' stand on the eastern side of the track, may have supported an auxiliary judges' stand.

121. Epidauros: Kavvadias, *op. cit.* (n. 105) Pls. A': γ, γ', δ; B': 6, 6'; Isthmia: Broneer, *op. cit.* (n. 96) 59, 140–42, Pls. 27d, 96; Corinth: C. H. Morgan, "Excavations at Corinth, 1936–1937," *AJA* 41 (1937) 550, Pls. XVI, XVII 1 foreground. Pausanias describes the *hysplex* in the hippodrome at Olympia (6.20.10–14).

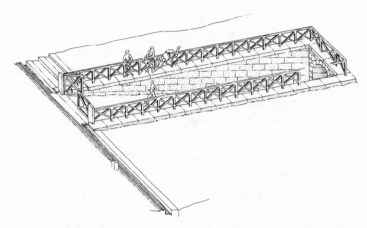

Fig. 65. Reconstructed perspective drawing of the entrance passageway, from the northeast.

The Entrance Tunnel

Approximately 20 m. north of the so-called auxiliary judges'
stand is a passageway leading to a vaulted tunnel, perpendicular to the line of the track, which was cut into the slope
on the western side of the Stadium. Since this slope steepens
toward the closed end of the Stadium, the placement of the
tunnel only 50 m. from the starting line increased the difficulty of construction considerably. Had it been located 100 m.
further north, for example, no tunnel (and no construction)
would have been necessary. The tunnel may have been situated to create a dramatic entrance for the athletes, who could
enter the Stadium amid the crowds extending along both
sides of the track (Fig. 65).[122]

122. Cf. the reference in Pausanias (6.20.8) to the "hidden entranceway"
(κρυπτὴ ἔσοδος) at Olympia; and Mallwitz, *op. cit.* (n. 62) 186–94, where the
traditional late Hellenistic or early Roman date is assigned to that tunnel. For the
entrance tunnel at Epidauros, see Patrucco, *op. cit.* (n. 105) Figs. XXII.1 and
XXV.1.

The Stadium entranceway connected with the Sacred Way to the west (which has not been excavated), which in turn led to the Temple of Zeus approximately 400 m. northwest of the Stadium. Athletes and judges coming from the sanctuary entered the Stadium through this tunnel, which also served as a dressing and waiting area for athletes. The tunnel itself is constructed of a sandy, relatively soft limestone and is well preserved for its entire original length of 36.35 m., although it has been necessary to replace missing blocks at its mouth with concrete and to brace one area from which a voussoir has fallen.

The vaulted tunnel and entranceway were constructed in the last quarter of the 4th century B.C. The relation of the south wall of the entranceway to the blocks of the sidewalk and water channel indicates that all these structures are contemporary. As we have already indicated on the basis of other evidence, the sidewalk and water channel were constructed in the late 4th century B.C. Pottery fragments from the third and fourth quarters of the 4th century, moreover, were found in the foundation trench for the south wall of the entranceway. Contemporary, or possibly earlier, parallels for the vaulted construction used in the entrance tunnel exist in Macedonian tombs.[123] It seems likely that the arch was first introduced to Greece as a result of Alexander's conquests in the East.[124] Construction of the entrance tunnel, therefore, may well have resulted from Macedonian influence at Nemea, as seen, for instance, in Cassander's presidency of the games of 315 B.C.,[125] which may have been responsible for the return of the games from Argos (see pp. 23, 40, 57–58). The Stadium and vaulted

---

123. See M. Andronicos, *Vergina: The Royal Tombs and the Ancient City* (Athens 1984) 31–37, 55–232, and 238–39, with bibliography to other tombs; see also R. A. Tomlinson, "Vaulting Techniques of the Macedonian Tombs," *APXAIA MAKEΔONIA* II (Thessaloniki 1977) 473–79.

124. T. D. Boyd, "The Arch and the Vault in Greek Architecture," *AJA* 82 (1978) 88–89.

125. Diodorus Siculus 19.64.1.

entranceway may thus be seen as part of the late 4th-century B.C. building program at Nemea, during which the Xenon, Bath, and Temple of Zeus were also constructed.

On each side of the mouth of the tunnel, a line of stone blocks extends almost 20 m. from the sidewalk to the eastern end of the tunnel. These blocks form the bottom courses of a retaining wall with flat coping blocks, which followed the slope of the hill to the top of the vault of the entrance tunnel (see Fig. 65). Ceramic evidence proves that the south wall of the entranceway collapsed before the 1st century after Christ, possibly as early as the late Hellenistic period,[126] crushing a nearby bronze statue or statues, almost two hundred fragments of which were found in the entranceway. These fragments include pieces of a hip, hair, and a wrist or ankle (museum case 7, p. 39). The subject of the statue or statues is uncertain. They may have depicted victors in the games, though at Olympia statues of Zeus (*Zanes*) were set up at the entrance to the stadium, paid for with the fines imposed on athletes who had taken bribes.[127]

By the 1st century after Christ, the central area of the entranceway had been partly cleared of the fallen stones and the rectilinear terracotta water channel installed.[128]

The face of the tunnel opening itself is unornamented, nor is there evidence to suggest that an ornamental facade originally existed. On each side of the tunnel a letter was carved into the eastern face of the first block, on the sixth course down from the keystone. On the north wall is a *chi,* on the south, a *delta.* The significance of these letters is uncertain. A hole cut at the corner of these same two blocks was probably used to hold a rope or chain across the tunnel entrance.

126. See *Hesperia* 48 (1979) 96. The blocks of the retaining wall which had fallen in have been lined up south of the entranceway.

127. See Pausanias 5.21.5; 6.2.6; 6.18.6.

128. The date of these developments is indicated by ceramic evidence, some of which is on display in museum case 10; see p. 44. See *Hesperia* 49 (1980) 198–99.

Fig. 66. Stadium tunnel graffito 1 63 (Akrotatos kalos).

The surface treatment of the courses of blocks in the tunnel varies considerably. The preserved surfaces of all nine courses of the vault are smoothly finished and preserve traces of stucco. (They provided an excellent surface on which to scratch graffiti.) In contrast, the surface of the fifth course down from the keystone was finished on both sides of the tunnel with a chisel 0.06 m. wide. This created almost vertical bands, separated by sharp ridges of stone. On the bottom four courses on both sides of the tunnel, a chisel 0.13 m. wide created horizontal rows with a horizontal ridge between each row. It also left vertical chisel marks from each individual stroke. The surfaces of the two side walls were treated after their construction, apparently for decoration, although the designs served as well to discourage graffiti at the level of these masonry courses.

Dozens of graffiti were scratched by athletes, often lightly, in the surface of the bottom two courses of the vault. In many of them a personal name is accompanied by the adjective *kalos,* "beautiful" or "fair." Several graffiti, moreover, can perhaps be identified with known individuals, including the name Telestas incised on the first block on the right (north) at the entrance to the tunnel (see p. 36).

Another noteworthy graffito is on the south wall about 9.50 m. from the eastern end of the tunnel. It is inscribed in crisp letters with the name Akrotatos. The same name (see p. 37) appears on the north wall 6.50 m. from the eastern end of the tunnel, on the third course down from the keystone. It is inscribed in bold letters 0.060–0.085 m. high (Fig. 66): "Akrotatos is beautiful". This rare name should probably be identified with the Spartan king Akrotatos, as already suggested.[129]

On the south wall of the tunnel approximately 8.00 m. from the eastern end, on the fourth course down from the keystone, are three superimposed graffiti, each in a distinct hand (Fig. 67). Toward the right side of the block is the earliest graffito, inscribed in letters 0.09 m. high. It has yet to be fully deciphered. Partly superimposed on these letters, and therefore later than them, is a graffito in which the lettering is neater and the strokes broader. Its letter height varies from 0.06 to 0.10 m., and it is legible as *Epikrates kalos,* "Epikrates is beautiful". At the upper left corner of the same block, a third graffito is inscribed in letters 0.025–0.035 m. high. Its late date is indicated by the relatively small amount of incrustation, its letter forms (e.g., the Ω is incised like a W),

129. This graffito may also be identified with the identically named grandfather of Akrotatos, who had died by 305 B.C. See Diodorus Siculus 19.70; Plutarch, *Agis* 3.4; Pausanias 1.13.5; 3.2–3.

Fig. 67.   Stadium tunnel graffito 1 52 (Epikrates, etc.).

and the Christian connotations of the name in question: Aitherizoes, "Ethereal life" (see p. 47).

This graffito was probably inscribed during the latest period of activity in the tunnel. The construction of the terracotta water channel in or before the 1st century after Christ was followed by a long period of abandonment, during which the ends of the tunnel silted up. The silt sloped downward toward the middle of the tunnel: the side walls are lighter in color where they were covered and protected by the silt. By

Fig. 68. Stadium tunnel graffito I 68 (Martialis).

removing the easternmost keystone and the voussoir blocks
flanking it, one or more persons subsequently entered the
tunnel and used it for shelter. The numerous animal bones
and fragments of cooking pottery found in the uppermost silt
in the tunnel provide evidence of this activity, which is dated
by numismatic evidence to the 570s or 580s after Christ (see
museum, p. 47, and Basilica, pp. 94–95).[130]

The tunnel has at present been cleared for a distance of
19 m. from its eastern end, at which point scaffolding has
been erected to support the vault. To reach the western end of
the tunnel, it is necessary to return to the Stadium track and,
just north of the Stadium entranceway, to proceed westward
some 55 m. across the top of the hill through which the
vaulted tunnel was cut. The western end of the tunnel, set
deep in the earth of the hillside, has an unornamented face,
like the eastern end. It also lacks the sloping walls that extend
from the eastern end of the tunnel to the edge of the Stadium
track.

130. See *Hesperia* 48 (1979) 99, and *Hesperia* 49 (1980) 200.

Approximately 1 m. inside the western end of the tunnel is another of the latest graffiti on the north wall, on the fourth course down from the keystone. The name Martialis is deeply carved with letters of Roman form 0.12 m. high (Fig. 68). This graffito probably dates from the 1st or 2nd century after Christ.

EPILOGUE

Any attempt to summarize or highlight the results of the excavation project at Nemea must include, among movable objects, the Classical marble relief (ss 8; see p. 30) and the bronze hydria (BR 379; see pp. 41–42). These pieces, from an art historical point of view, give much to our understanding of their periods. The same can be said on the architectural side for the fragments of the Early Temple of Zeus (case 19; see pp. 57–60) and for the Stadium entrance tunnel (pp. 184–91). The latter adds additional insights thanks to the graffiti on its walls.

More important, the coins, broken bits and pieces of pottery, architecture, inscriptions, figurines, and the like have sharpened our picture of Nemea considerably as we have come to understand, for example, that this sacrosanct Panhellenic center suffered a violent destruction late in the 5th century B.C. and that the Nemean Games were repeatedly moved back and forth between Argos and Nemea. Indeed, we now know that those games, which endured for more than a millennium as an institution, actually took place at Nemea for less than a quarter of that time. In other words, Nemea shows us that peace in the ancient world was an elusive goal. The Panhellenic impulse did meet with considerable success, but it also encountered problems, and some of these have been more clearly defined at Nemea. Solutions—whether successful or not—to those problems in ancient Greece provide lessons in international relations for our society. It would be a happy result of the Nemea project if we have made those lessons more widely known.

Perhaps the nicest lesson of the project, however, has been that there are so many people curious about our common heritage and willing to support archaeological research in an effort to satisfy that curiosity. Since 1973 the Nemea project has been funded largely (about 90 percent) by the gifts of private citizens and foundations. Those who supported the excavations during the first decade of the project have been acknowledged by a marble plaque in the museum (see p. 17). Those who supported the reconstruction of the Temple of Zeus during that same period were acknowledged in the catalogue for the exhibition at the Benaki Museum in Athens in April 1983. It seems appropriate to conclude this book by acknowledging those who since 1983 have made it possible for our research to continue and for this book to be published. We acknowledge their support with sincere gratitude and, in many cases, deep affection.

Tom and Billie Long

BENEFACTORS

Anonymous
Moore Dry Dock Foundation
National Pro-Am Youth Fund

SPONSORS

Mary I. Baldwin
Robert L. and Alice Bridges
Bill and Jennifer Langan
Phyllis Wattis

PATRONS

David and Howard Allen

The Trustees of the American
    School of Classical Studies
    at Athens
Carlo and Eleanor Anderson
John and Barbara Bellamy
Norma and Alexander Cantin
Charles and Lila Carmichael
Dolly Bright Carter
Marjory Farquhar
Jerry and Millie FitzGerald
Peter and Robin Frazier
Albert and Carol Gentner
Patricia L. Golton
Dorothy M. Kesseli
Ted and Phyllis Kiernan

Maurice and Arlene King
In memoriam James N. Kirkwood
Mr. and Mrs. Melvin B. Lane
Jok and Kirsten Legallet
Patricia Hall Lott
Stephen G. Miller
Donald and Mary Mitchell
Jim and Jane Moore
Jack and Dede Nickel
Mr. and Mrs. Richard C. Otter
Rudolph and Barbara Peterson
Neville and Lila Rich
Thomas L. Shelton
R. Scott and Gretchen W.
  Sherman
Nancy P. Weston
Garff B. Wilson

CONTRIBUTORS

Dorothy André
Mr. and Mrs. Clark A. Barrett
Natalie Pyle Barton
John Archibald Calhoun
Earl and June Cheit
E. Morris Cox
Dick and Jan Erickson
Jack and Iris Farr
Jim and Susan Fousekis
Richard and Elizabeth Hall
Carl and Betty Helmholz
Mr. and Mrs. Charles F. Lowrey
Theodore B. Lyman
John and Mary Macmeeken
Mr. and Mrs. Harry F. McCrea
Steve R. Mahaffy

Elizabeth S. Mitchum
Vincent S. Mulford
Mr. and Mrs. David P. Myers
Richard and Marianne Peterson
Nicholas and Patricia Petrakis
Thorndike and Janet Saville
Jim and Janice Vohs
Mr. and Mrs. Robert A. Wertsch
Virginia Perry Wilson

DONORS

Leland D. Adams, Jr.
In memoriam June Alexander
Steve Allen
William and Aliki Ammerman
Mr. and Mrs. Darrell and
  Miss Ellen Amyx
Andersen Travel Ltd.
Harry and Jane Andersen
Mr. and Mrs. J. K. Anderson
Kinsey and Lilica Anderson
Ward and Elaine Anderson
Diogenes J. Angelakos
Fani Antoniadou
Frank and Lucille Asaro
Rosemary M. Barnwell
Lynne A. Bauer
Jeffrey W. Baus
Walter and Evelyn Bell
Helen Benda
Mel and Ella Bennington
William and Dorothy Biddick
Bing Fund Corporation
D. Birge
Jane S. Birge

Mr. and Mrs. Armand D. Bosc
Phyllis Bosley
Al and Rose Bowker
Frances V. Bristol
Dyke Brown Family Trust
Max and Nancy Burchett
Elizabeth M. Butterworth
Frances Koster Byford
Arthur and Helene Cevasco
Michael and Alice Chetkovich
James H. Clark
Robert and Frances Connick
Patricia S. Cotton
Ann and Floyd Criswell
Peter T. Dalis
Dr. and Mrs. Aubrey M. Davis
Robert and Judith Davis
John and Mary Delistraty
Vernon DeMars
Frank and Almira De Pace
John and Jean Dillon
Agnes L. Dimitriou
Yvonne Dolan
Theodore and Elizabeth Durein
Ted and Georgia Econome
Ralph and Barbara Edwards
Sanford S. Elberg
Arthur and Christine England
Dr. and Mrs. Seymour M. Farber
Marie Fontenrose
August and Susan Frugé
Diana V. Gardener
Monte and Helen Getler
Darthula Gibbins
Vernon and Marion Goodin

Chauncey and Doris Goodrich
Glen and Gail Grant
Shirley M. Greig
Mrs. Eloise Foote Halperin
Janice Hamilton
Clyde and Margaret Henry
James H. Hicks
Omer and Nancy Hirst
Charles J. Hitch
Bill and Beverly Holloman
Richard and Constance Holton
Mr. and Mrs. R. B. Honeyman
Helen L. Hurst
Dick and Mary Jencks
David N. and Vannie T.
   Keightley
Parker and Margaret Kemp
Van Dusen Kennedy
Robert and Carolyn Knapp
Henry and Evelyn Knoll
Dr. Joel J. Kudler
Joseph T. and Martha L. Jurick
Mr. and Mrs. Lewis K. Land
Ellen St. Sure Lifschutz
Jim and Marjorie Luce
Mr. and Mrs. Birke Luckenbill
Chester and Nina McCorkle
Edwin and Nancy Marks
Don and Joan Mastronarde
Beecher Mathes
Birdie A. Mayes
Mr. and Mrs. Gaylord W. Miller
Barbara Morrill
Martin Morrison
John and Mignette Najarian

Walter and Gloria Olson
Charles and Catherine Page
Costas and Thetis Pappas
Kalliope Paraskevopoulou
Edith C. Parker
Harriet T. Parsons
Margaret S. Philbrook
Mr. and Mrs. John Pillsbury
Charles Pisciotta
Antony and Isabelle Raubitschek
Patricia L. Reilly
Lenore Hennessey Richardson
Linda Riley
Laurie Rohrer
Tom and Lilo Rosenmeyer
John C. Sandberg
Virginia Caswell Sherwin
Virginia Carter Sholl
Mrs. Howard B. Shontz
Gene and Betty Shurtleff
Earl and Virginia Simburg
Mary-Ellen Sougey
William W. Sterling
Ron and Connie Stroud
Ann Stutts
Apollo and Johanna Taleporos
Patricia and William Taylor
George and Rosemary
   Tchobanoglous
George and Helena Thacher
Wilbur and Dorothy Thomas

Homer and Dorothy Thompson
Robert and Terry Tough
Betty Trotter
George P. Turner
Peter W. Van der Naillen
Lucille Vlahos
Jan and Jeannie de Vries
Dr. and Mrs. Gilbert Allen Webb
Marjorie C. Willcox
Roy B. Woolsey
Lou Zaharopoulos

SUPPORTERS OF THE TEMPLE OF ZEUS RECONSTRUCTION 1983–1988

Alex G. Spanos

CONTRIBUTORS

Forrest and Shirley Plant
John and Tina Siambis

DONORS

Kenneth R. Abraham
Patricia Aleck
George and Panagiota Bonorris
Lavelle Hanna
Soterios and Fifi Menzelos
Dr. and Mrs. Frank G. Nicholas
Nick and Anna Petris

BIBLIOGRAPHIC
ABBREVIATIONS

AA	*Archäologischer Anzeiger*
AJA	*American Journal of Archaeology*
Ἀρχ. Δελτ.	*Ἀρχαιολογικὸν Δελτίον, Χρονικά*
Ἀρχ. Ἐφ.	*Ἀρχαιολογικὴ Ἐφημερίς*
BCH	*Bulletin de correspondance hellénique*
BEFAR	*Bibliothèque des écoles françaises d'Athènes et de Rome*
Βιβλ. Ἀθ. Ἀρχ. Ἑτ.	*Βιβλιοθήκη τῆς ἐν Ἀθῆναις Ἀρχαιολογικῆς Ἑταιρείας*
CSCA	*California Studies in Classical Antiquity*
G&R	*Greece and Rome*
IG	*Inscriptiones graecae*
JHS	*Journal of Hellenic Studies*
LIMC	*Lexicon iconographicum mythologiae classicae*
LSJ⁹	Liddell, H. G., Scott, R., and Jones, H. S. *A Greek-English Lexicon*. 9th edition (Oxford 1940)
RendLinc	*Rendiconti della reale accademia dei Lincei*
SEG	*Supplementum epigraphicum graecum*
ZPE	*Zeitschrift für Papyrologie und Epigraphik*

BIBLIOGRAPHY

This bibliography includes only modern material directly relevant to Nemea. It is intended to lead the interested reader to specialized studies or to the preliminary reports of the excavations. The symbol † indicates a posthumous publication.

L. Bacchielli, "L'adyton del Tempio di Zeus a Nemea," *RendLinc* ser. 8: 37 (1982) 219–37.

C. W. Blegen, "The American Excavation at Nemea, Season of 1924," *Art and Archaeology* 19 (1925) 175–84.

———, "The December Excavations at Nemea," *Art and Archaeology* 22 (1926) 127–34, 139.

———, "Excavations at Nemea, 1926," *AJA* 31 (1927) 421–40.

†C. W. Blegen, "Neolithic Remains at Nemea," *Hesperia* 44 (1975) 251–79.

D. W. Bradeen, "Inscriptions from Nemea," *Hesperia* 35 (1966) 320–30.

O. Broneer, "The Isthmian Victory Crown," *AJA* 66 (1962) 259–63.

M. Clemmensen and R. Vallois, "Le Temple de Zeus à Némée," *BCH* 49 (1925) 1–20.

F. A. Cooper, S[tella] G. Miller, S[tephen] G. Miller, and C. Smith, *The Temple of Zeus at Nemea: Perspectives and Prospects* (Athens 1983).

H. N. Couch, "An Inscribed Votive Bronze Bull," *AJA* 35 (1931) 44–47.

G. Cousin and F. Dürrbach, "Inscriptions de Némée," *BCH* 9 (1885) 349–56.

D. J. Geagan, "Inscriptions from Nemea," *Hesperia* 37 (1968) 381–85.

J. P. Harland, "The Excavations of Tsoungiza, the Prehistoric Site of Nemea," *AJA* 32 (1928) 63.

F. D. Harvey, "A Nemean Metagraffito," *AJA* 86 (1982) 586.

————, "Second Thoughts on the Nemean Metagraffito," *AJA* 88 (1984) 70.

†B. H. Hill, *The Temple of Zeus at Nemea* (Princeton 1966).

S[tella] G. Miller, "A Miniature Athena Promachos," *Hesperia,* Suppl. 20 (1982) 93–99.

————, "Excavations at Nemea, 1982," *Hesperia* 52 (1983) 70–95.

————, "Excavations at Nemea, 1983," *Hesperia* 53 (1984) 171–92.

————, "Archaic Relief Wares from the Nemea Area," ΦΙΛΙΑ ΕΠΗ II (Festsch. Mylonas, Athens 1988) 266–84.

————, "Excavations at the Panhellenic Site of Nemea: Cults, Politics, and Games," *The Archaeology of the Olympics* (Madison 1988) 141–51.

S[tephen] G. Miller, "Excavations at Nemea, 1973–1974," *Hesperia* 44 (1975) 143–72.

————, "The Pentathlon for Boys at Nemea," *CSCA* 8 (1975) 199–201.

————, "New Problems at Nemea," *Neue Forschungen in griechischen Heiligtümern* (Tübingen 1976) 63–75.

————, "Excavations at Nemea, 1975," *Hesperia* 45 (1976) 174–202.

————, "Excavations at Nemea, 1976," *Hesperia* 46 (1977) 1–26.

————, "Excavations at Nemea, 1977," *Hesperia* 47 (1978) 58–88.

————, "Excavations at Nemea, 1978," *Hesperia* 48 (1979) 73–103.

————, "Excavations at Nemea, 1979," *Hesperia* 49 (1980) 178–205.

————, "Tunnel Vision: The Nemean Games," *Archaeology* 33 (1980) 54–56.

————, "Excavations at Nemea, 1980," *Hesperia* 50 (1981) 45–67.

————, "Excavations at Nemea, 1981," *Hesperia* 51 (1982) 19–40.

————, "Kleonai, the Nemean Games, and the Lamian War," *Hesperia,* Suppl. 20 (1982) 100–108.

————, "Poseidon at Nemea," ΦΙΛΙΑ ΕΠΗ I (Festsch. Mylonas, Athens, 1986), 261–71.

————, "Excavations at Nemea, 1984–1986," *Hesperia* 57 (1988) 1–20.

————, "The Theorodokoi of the Nemean Games," *Hesperia* 57 (1988) 147–63.

L. Pearson, "The Fair Akrotatos from Nemea," *AJA* 88 (1984) 69–70.

W. Pülhorn, "Archemoros," *LIMC* II (Zurich 1984) 472–75.

D. G. Romano, "The Early Stadium at Nemea," *Hesperia* 46 (1977) 27–31.

E. Simon, "Archemoros," *AA* (1979) 31–45.

R. S. Stroud, "An Argive Decree from Nemea," *Hesperia* 53 (1984) 193–216.

C. K. Williams, "Nemea," *Ἀρχ. Δελτ.* 20 (1965) *Χρον.* 154–56.

I. Worthington, "The Nemean 'Akrotatos the Good' Again," *AJA* 90 (1986) 41.

J. C. Wright, "Excavations at Tsoungiza (Archaia Nemea), 1981," *Hesperia* 51 (1982) 375–97.

INDEX